The Kingdom Strikes Back

The Kingdom Strikes Back

Signs of the Messiah at Work

by
Howard Culbertson

Nazarene Publishing House
Kansas City, Missouri

10   9   8   7   6   5   4   3   2   1

Contents

Foreword

It has been especially satisfying to me to have been personally involved in the missionary career of Howard Culbertson. I was privileged to be a part of the process that sent Howard and his wife to their first overseas assignment. Since then, I have watched them serve God and the church efficiently and effectively. The worldwide church has further benefited from the exceptional writing skills of this missionary. Howard's ability with the pen first surfaced when he was a student in college. He has continued to develop his talent so that now there are many of us who eagerly await his next article or book.

When I received a copy of the manuscript *The Kingdom Strikes Back,* I set it aside to read while on an overseas trip. I began reading it on a flight between Djakarta, Indonesia, and Hong Kong. I found that I was unable to lay it down until I had read every word. By chance, a Nazarene lady from Arlington, Va., was on that same flight, sitting just across the aisle from me. I suggested that she might enjoy the manuscript as well. It turned out to be a joyful reading experience—almost a competition—as she was always just a page or two behind me, enjoying it as much as I. It was a seven-mile-high Nazarene missionary study lesson that allowed fellow passengers to get glimpses into Nazarene missions as we exchanged pages and comments.

But *The Kingdom Strikes Back* is more than a story on missionary work. Howard has based his book on a unique and powerful interpretation of New Testament truth regarding the kingdom of God. The book provides devotional as well as thoughtful reading.

Thanks, Howard, for another contribution to the missionary reading list. Already we are looking forward to your next one. In the midst of your busy schedule may you find time to keep your pen writing and your thoughts flowing. You contribute greatly to our missionary interest by doing so.

JERALD D. JOHNSON

1

The Kingdom Strikes Back

Senseless violence. Starving children. Guns firing in anger and fear. AIDS epidemic. Polluted water. Hate and racism. Dehumanizing abuse.

Those are the words in today's frightful newspaper headlines. Sadly, the datelines for such news could be from almost any country in the world—including Haiti, where we've been missionaries. Television news often shows us a world seething with pain, chaos, treachery, and abuse.

The world wasn't always so rotten. On the sixth day of creation, God looked at what He had made. The Bible says that what He saw was "very good" (Gen. 1:31). Indeed, it was good. In many ways it still is.

Years ago the Billy Graham Crusades introduced us to a Swedish song we know as "How Great Thou Art." The first verse expounds the believer's awe as he sees creation's marvels. Don't you like that song? I like it in English. I like it in Italian. I like it in Haitian Creole. In whatever language I've learned it, that song's message always thrills me.

Haiti's flame-red flamboyant trees, its mango trees festooned with ripe fruit, the tiny hummingbirds darting around hibiscus blossoms—all show the Creator's artistic tastes. Haiti's coastal waters contain some of the most beautiful coral reefs in the world.

God did create a very good world. Yet some ghastly scars

mar the marvels of God's creation. It began in the Garden of Eden, an earthly paradise. There, man was to live forever in close communion with his Creator. Unfortunately, Adam and Eve didn't stay content as created beings. Following the tempter's suggestion, they sought to become like God, to become complete in themselves. Their revolt unleashed a chaotic train of events that scarred not only man but also the whole universe.

Following Adam and Eve's monstrous choice, things like death, hatred and anguish, isolation and emptiness invaded "normal" life. Even worse, God's image in human beings was horribly defaced. Because of their estrangement from God, things not part of created human nature now seem "natural." A crippling spiritual disease attacked the very center of human selfhood. The apostle Paul described the resulting corruption as "the carnal nature" (see Rom. 7:14; 8:6, 7, KJV).

Following Adam and Eve's disobedience, sin's depraving power snowballed. In a fit of rage, Adam and Eve's son, Cain, killed his brother. Sometime later, his descendant, Lamech, killed another man. He moved beyond Cain's fear of discovery to near boastfulness over the murder. Seeming to revel in snuffing out a human life, Lamech dared the world to do something about it (Gen. 4:23-24). Nor did it end there. Through the centuries man has sunk lower and lower under sin's hardening power.

That's tragic. Humankind was God's crowning act of creation. Even today there's still evidence of that. The rich cultural traditions of Haiti are a delightful treat for tourists. That's true also of Zambia or Peru or New Zealand. The photographers of *National Geographic* traipse around the globe, thrilling us with photos of the exotic and colorful. That inward bent toward sin that was caused by Adam and Eve's disobedience has, however, led people of every age and of every culture to fill their lives "with every kind of wickedness, evil, greed and depravity" (Rom. 1:29).

Our plight as depraved sinners shouts at us from the pages of daily newspapers from Boston to Bangkok. Even utopia-minded historians concede man's inhumanity to man. Sociologists and psychologists ponder sin's corroding effects (even if they refuse to call it "sin").

While the history of any nation can easily illustrate sin's cataclysmic effects, let's take Haiti as our "Exhibit A." This small nation lies just east of Cuba on the western third of a mountainous island called Hispaniola. It was this island that Christopher Columbus discovered in 1492.

Spanish settlers followed Columbus to Hispaniola. They tried enslaving the native Arawak Indians. As you might expect, some of the Indians resisted losing their freedom. They were slaughtered on the spot. The rest of their fellow tribesmen began dying from gross maltreatment. From the first page of Haiti's modern history thus oozes the ruthlessness that Rom. 1:31 associates with godless man.

Things did not improve in Haiti. French pirates arrived, hiding in coastal coves. Some started plantations of sugar, coffee, cocoa, indigo, and cotton. Plantations needed lots of cheap labor. By then the Indians had all died. So these Frenchmen headed for Africa to recruit workers at gunpoint. At the height of the West Indies slave trade, more than 700 ships regularly crisscrossed the Atlantic. Their cargo? Chained human beings. For thousands of Africans, a tropical paradise dissolved into a living hell.

In the late 1700s those slaves successfully revolted against their French masters. Tragically, even liberty from colonial masters did not stop the bloodshed. Repeated periods of civil unrest, brutal kings, and cruel dictators led one American couple to write a history of Haiti called *Written in Blood.* Another author poignantly says that Haiti is a country "whose soil has drunk more blood than sweat."

Adam's cosmic treason shattered his close ties to his Creator. The aftermath of his fall poisoned relationships between people. It also damaged the natural world in ways we still don't understand. With the Fall, the whole cosmos—in addition to man's heart—became riddled with evil and the spirit of rebellion. I don't believe that sin directly causes all human suffering. Yet the anguish caused by disease and natural disasters is somehow linked to sin's curse. Because of man's sin, Paul writes, the universe is in "bondage to decay" (Rom. 8:21). The diseases plaguing Haiti today—malaria, tuberculosis, hepatitis, gastrointestinal problems—were unknown in the Garden of Eden. Before their fall, neither drought nor typhoons nor flash floods troubled Adam and Eve.

Furthermore, human beings have caused a progressive deterioration of their own environment. Ecologists tell us that we have irreparably spoiled parts of this planet. They say we've fouled our own nest!

Sin's double-whammy blows to the moral quality of life and the physical environment show up clearly in Haiti. Plagues of disease, soil erosion, overpopulation, illiteracy, poverty, and superstition cloud the future of every newborn Haitian. To many, Haiti's plight looks futile. Haiti seems so hopeless that one international commission labeled it a "bottomless pit" for foreign aid efforts. This prestigious group recommended ending all outside help to Haiti.

What a dismal picture! There is, however, some good news for this troubled world and its human tenants. When God ejected Adam and Eve from the Garden of Eden, He did not desert them. Their sin may have wrought terrible havoc and ruin. Still, there soon shone a glimmer of hope.

The shock waves of their disobedience were still shaking the universe when God promised a Redeemer (Gen. 3:15). As God passed judgment on Adam and Eve, He also held out a promise. His kingdom, He said, would be striking back. He had a plan to undo the fateful results of their fall. In the end His hosts from heaven would put to flight every enemy of divine rule.

It took a while. Then one starry night in a little village south of Jerusalem, the promise began to be fulfilled. In an animal shed near Bethlehem the kingdom of God reentered this sinful world. A few years later God incarnate in Jesus emerged from a Nazareth carpentry shop. Setting the stage for His ministry had been His cousin, John. John's own prophetic ministry was brief but powerful. His major theme: The long-promised Messiah would soon appear. That Messiah, he said, was a man of fire who would inaugurate a new kingdom.

When He was ready to begin His public ministry, Jesus found John down at the Jordan River and asked him for baptism. That day God used John the Baptist to announce that the promised Messiah had arrived. But then months and years passed, and Jesus did not become the hoped-for political savior. Nor did He march into the Temple and take over as a new Jewish religious leader.

This disappointed some. Those who watched Him closely, however, marveled at His potent power over nature. That, coupled with the masterful way He spoke, convinced many that God's kingdom had indeed invaded the world. The strong and mighty overlooked it, but God's kingdom had begun striking back.

Meanwhile, John's bold charges of sexual sin in the palace landed him in prison. Prison is a dreary place. Your mind can play tricks on you there. Languishing in a dungeon at Machaerus, John's mind returned to a spot in the Jordan River valley.

There he had proclaimed Jesus as the Messiah. Now a tiny doubt crept in. Was Jesus really the Anointed One? Knowing he might soon die, John craved reassurance. So he asked some of his close followers to investigate again.

Going directly to Jesus, they asked point-blank: "Are You the One who was to come?" In response, Jesus did not say a simple "Yes" or "No." He pointed instead to the wondrous things happening in His ministry.

"Go tell John," He told them, "that the blind are receiving sight. Tell him that the crippled are walking. The deaf are hearing. The lepers are being cured, and the disinherited of the earth are having the gospel preached to them" (paraphrase of Matt. 11:5 and Luke 7:22).

Old Testament prophets had said that the Messiah's coming would be accompanied by just such miracles. Jesus pointed to the miracles in His ministry, leaving John and his disciples to draw their own conclusions.

After only three years of a ministry featuring these kinds of miracles, Jewish religious leaders arrested Jesus and quickly put Him to death. Three days later He rose from the dead. Six weeks after that, He ascended into heaven.

Now what would happen? Jesus was no longer present in bodily form. Perhaps the miracles would disappear. They did not. That should not surprise us. Jesus himself had promised that the signs would continue. He even said they would increase. After all, the Kingdom had come. On the night before His crucifixion, He tried to prepare His 11 remaining disciples for the future. One of the things He said was that His followers would do "even greater things" than He had done (John 14:12).

So it has been. After Jesus' ascension, Spirit-filled believers scattered across the globe. They went preaching and teaching the good news of the Kingdom. Wherever they went, God's mighty works revealed His power. Through the years,

a day. Many go home proudly wearing used glasses collected by people like my mother. For sight-impaired Haitians, the gift of clear vision received from Dr. Gamertsfelder is a real miracle of the Kingdom.

There are, to be sure, documented cases of God intervening dramatically in Haiti to restore full sight to blinded eyes. During Jesus' earthly ministry, healing sometimes came that way. He simply spoke. His words were enough to make men whole. Other times Jesus chose to touch the diseased or defective part. He put His hand on a leper. He stuck His fingers in the ears of a deaf man. He touched the eyes of a blind man.

Today, God still works both ways to heal physical blindness. Sometimes He intervenes dramatically. At other times He uses the dedicated hands of men like Paul Gamertsfelder. In either case, whether by His word alone or through the touch of a Kingdom envoy, it's time for praise and adoration.

"The Blind People That Have Eyes"

Physical blindness can handicap a person. Other kinds of blindness, however, wreak greater havoc. The confusion—even terror—reigning across the globe today is evidence of a spiritually blind world. Zephaniah foretold of sinners who would "walk like blind men," vainly groping and stumbling along (1:17).

In 1955 a young Haitian army officer walked into a service at the Avenue Dessalines Church of the Nazarene. Duroc Placide responded to what he saw, heard, and felt in the church. Captivated by the presence and work of the Holy Spirit in that church, he soon gave his heart to the Lord.

Within a short time Duroc began showing some leadership gifts. He played a role in planting a new church on the other side of Port-au-Prince in a suburb called Martissant. He began praying about a call to preach. By 1960 Duroc was certain of God's call to the ministry, so he enrolled in Haiti's Nazarene Bible Institute in the foothills above Port-au-Prince.

Upon graduation a church called him as pastor. From the start he was a dynamic leader. So three years later when Avenue Dessalines, where he was converted, was looking for a new pastor, they turned to him.

After some fruitful pastorates, he felt led to spend a couple of years in full-time evangelism. Then he helped found the church at Cap Haitien, a major city and Haiti's old colonial capital on the north coast. In 1977 the Haiti North District capped Duroc Placide's ministerial career by electing him district superintendent.

Duroc Placide led the North District to redouble its church planting and outreach efforts. By 1984 it needed to be divided into three separate districts. Rev. Placide became superintendent of one of those new districts. That year he also spearheaded a drive for simultaneous baptismal services in Nazarene churches across Haiti. His fervor and urging led Haitian Nazarene pastors to baptize 2,749 people on the last Sunday of September 1984.

Sounds like a terrific, successful life, doesn't it? It is. There's just one sour note in it. Like the apostle Paul, Rev. Placide had his "thorn in the flesh" (2 Cor. 12:7, KJV). Through years of successful evangelism, church planting, and district leadership Rev. Placide was slowly going blind. Finally, at the apex of his career, total darkness closed in on him.

Duroc's sight problems began while he was in the Haitian military. One day a horse threw him. When his head hit the ground, the blow damaged the sight center of his brain. His eyesight started slowly deteriorating. Doctors tried unsuccessfully to halt the degeneration. The general church even provided air transportation for him to see an eye specialist in

Florida. It was too late. Irreparable damage had been done. Furthermore, nothing could be done to stop its continued deterioration. Nazarenes began sending concerts of prayer heavenward on his behalf. Still the darkness continued closing in. Finally Duroc Placide went totally blind.

Paul of Tarsus had an impairment of some kind too. We don't know for sure what it was. He simply called it a "thorn in the flesh." Though he prayed intensely for the removal of that thorn, God did not take it away. Instead, He told Paul that the problem (whatever it was) would remain. Its presence would reveal the strength of the risen Christ. In a similar way, Rev. Placide's defective vision has shown how human weakness can pave the way for God's grace and power.

I've watched that blind preacher carefully make his way up and down rocky mountain trails visiting churches. At his elbow was always a young pastor. That young pastor became his eyes on those trails, helping him over boulders and around tree roots. In 1987 Duroc Placide retired. Physical healing never came to his eyes. With the passing years, however, his spiritual vision became clearer and clearer. When Duroc Placide stepped into the pulpit or met around a table with church leaders, all uncertainty and tentativeness disappeared. What a powerful spiritual leader he was.

He still holds revival meetings, helping those whose spiritual and moral blindness is more tragic than his physical blindness. They are "the blind people that have eyes" of which Isaiah spoke (43:8, KJV).

I've rejoiced as I've listened to young pastors testify to Rev. Placide's key role in their decision to become preachers. Today, men influenced by Rev. Duroc Placide fill the pulpits of several Nazarene churches in Haiti. Through this one blind man, the Kingdom has brought sight to many. The blind are seeing. The Messiah has come!

The Blindness of Illiteracy

Few nations have lower literacy rates than Haiti. Even the most optimistic reports say that no more than 20 percent of the Haitians over age 15 can read and write. There are historical, religious, and economic reasons for this.

When the French colonists brought thousands of Africans in chains to Haiti, the only interest they had in those slaves was their muscle power. They did nothing to educate them. Slave owners even tried to prohibit their slaves from learning to read and write. Then the unthinkable happened. In 1791 a slave revolt broke out in northern Haiti. Napoleon's armies could not quell it. Ten years of bloody struggle followed. Finally, the slaves forced their French masters to withdraw, climaxing the first successful slave rebellion in history. They were, however, a nation of illiterates.

While the Haitians won their political independence, they remained culturally tied to France. Only a tiny minority of Haitians ever mastered the French language. Still, French language and culture were placed on a pedestal. If you craved social status, you had to speak French. Haitians who spoke only Creole, an oral language, were looked down upon. Such cultural and linguistic snobbery created a tiny elite who knew French. The masses who spoke only Creole remained illiterate. Until the middle of this century, no one bothered to put Creole in written form. Only when a Methodist missionary turned oral Creole into a written language did the literacy door finally begin to creak open for Haiti.

Almost every one of Haiti's constitutions has decreed compulsory education. Unfortunately, the government has never found the money to carry out that mandate. In addition, Haiti's chief religion, voodoo, has no sacred book. Thus it does not provide a stimulus either to learn to read or to produce printed material in Haitian's heart language. How different from Christianity, whose converts hunger to learn to read from God's Book!

Not being able to read gives you a kind of blindness. You may have eyes, but your brain cannot interpret what you see on the printed page. As far as comprehending, you may as well be blind. Unless you can read, you are walled off from technological advances, from important health and medical advice, from agricultural breakthroughs. Even God's written Word has no power for you unless someone reads it aloud to you.

When these scales of illiteracy drop from your eyes, that's a miracle! In Haiti today miracle-working literacy programs are restoring sight. The Kingdom is striking back. God is using the efforts of Nazarenes to open new horizons of the printed word to thousands of people. Nazarenes in Haiti fight the blindness of illiteracy on two fronts: with adults and with children. The largest and most consistent effort is that of our programs for helping children learn to read and write.

The Little Children and Jesus

On several occasions Jesus used children to illustrate a message about the Kingdom. Perhaps the best-known is Matt. 19:14. There Jesus says, "Let the children come to me; do not try to stop them; for the kingdom of Heaven belongs to such as these" (NEB).

Children are special to the ministry of the Church of the Nazarene in Haiti. Almost everywhere the church has gone in that Caribbean nation, a school has been started. One school is even named the Phineas F. Bresee Elementary School. This concern for educating children stands in stark contrast to voodooism. That religion sponsors no elementary schools. Each of the 250 Nazarene elementary schools is a sign that the Kingdom is invading Haiti with power. There's also one Nazarene-sponsored high school in Port-au-Prince with the hopes of launching another one or two soon. About 25,000 Haitian children study in these schools. That's more than we have in any other country.

Few of these schools have decent buildings. Most have only dirt floors. The students sit on simple wooden benches. Flimsy pieces of Masonite hardboard serve as chalkboards. Unfortunately the demand for schools has far outstripped the number of trained teachers. In isolated mountain villages, any adult who can read may wind up as a schoolteacher.

That's not ideal. It's bad educational philosophy. It's bad pedagogy. Even in less-than-ideal conditions, however, the blind are beginning to see. Rural Haitians whose high rates of illiteracy blinded them now begin to see. Dawn is breaking in on darkened understandings.

Even though these schools face enormous problems, we are making progress in improving their quality. We now have a university-trained specialist helping elevate the schools educationally. He organizes in-service training opportunities for teachers. He also is the Nazarene spokesperson in government education offices.

One of the things we're doing to help our schools is that of providing hot lunches. The majority of parents cannot pay more than a minimal tuition to send their children to school. Sometimes even $1.00 per month is prohibitive in a country where per capita annual income is about $350. Little government support is available. There are, however, several groups working in Haiti to help schools and particularly to subsidize hot lunch programs. Several of these are helping Nazarene schools. These include Compassion International, CARE, Church World Service, and a Dutch group called Word and Action.

Recently, Nazarene Compassionate Ministries started a Nazarene Child Sponsorship program. Nazarenes in North

America and Europe are helping sponsor school hot lunch programs in Haiti. In return they get a photo of the children in that school and a description of what their help is doing. At present about 100 Nazarene schools have hot lunch sponsors.

As I look back on my own childhood, I remember my mother drilling into me the importance of proper nourishment. Eating right would help me do well in school, she said. So people sponsoring hot lunches for Haitian Nazarene schoolchildren invest in both nutrition and education.

The Kingdom is striking back. The blind are beginning to see—and they're getting a good lunch too!

A Rustling in the Treetops

Remember the Philistines? They were real troublemakers. David had just been anointed king when those Philistines "went up in full force to search for him" (2 Sam. 5:17). Having the Philistines bother them was nothing new for Israel. From the time Joshua crossed the Jordan River, these "Sea People" had been a constant menace. Now, by occupying the Rephaim Valley between Jerusalem and Bethlehem, they challenged David directly.

After a seesaw standoff King David sought the Lord's guidance. The Lord told him to have his soldiers take up attack positions. Then they were to wait for "a rustling sound" (NEB) "in the tops of the balsam trees" (2 Sam. 5:24). That noise would mean the Lord and His heavenly hosts were leading the way into battle. When that sound came, "Move quickly," the Lord told David. It would signal that the victory belonged to God's people.

That's what happened. In that battle, Israel shattered the Philistine forces. Never again did they seriously threaten Israel. As promised, those rustling sounds in the treetops foretold complete victory for God's people.

I've heard rustling sounds in Haiti's spiritual battlefields. Those sounds tell me that God still leads the way into battle. For me they are sure signs that God's army continues to win victories. One such rustling sound I hear comes from pages turning in Bibles and New Testaments. It's a sound I've often heard in churches all across Haiti.

As noted earlier, even the most encouraging literacy figures say 80 percent of the Haitians over age 15 cannot read or write. Contrasting with that dismal figure is the fact that in many Haitian Churches of the Nazarene more than half of the members *are* literate. That's a literacy rate *nearly three times* that of the general population. Motivating Christians to learn to read is, of course, the ability to read the Bible. For most Haitian believers a Bible or New Testament becomes one of their most prized possessions.

Once I sat in our Pétionville church, located in the foothills above Port-au-Prince. There, each week Sunday School closes with a statistical report. Among the figures they give is the number of Bibles and New Testaments in church that day. On this particular Sunday—a very ordinary Sunday—216 people came to Sunday School. Number of Bible and New Testaments? *One hundred and forty-nine!* That day 7 of every 10 people had brought a Bible or New Testament to church. Later in the worship service the pastor announced his Scripture reading. I listened to that beautiful rustling of pages softly echoing off the corrugated tin roofing.

As I listened to those rustling pages, I wanted to jump up on the pew and shout, "Hallelujah!" Visitors to Haiti today watch it reeling from political, economic, and ecological ills. To a country like that, the Lord's coming in power and strength is good news. That rustling in church told me that God was leading His people to battle. The blindness of illiteracy gives way to people reading God's Word for themselves.

The writer of Hebrews reminds us: "The word of God is living and active. Sharper than any double-edged sword" (Heb. 4:12). Not long ago the Lord made it possible for us to put 30,000 of these weapons in Haitian hands. It began in 1984. That year a Florida group gave us about 6,000 Creole New Testaments. Then, in the latter part of 1986, Bible Literature International helped us buy 10,000 more New Testaments to give away. In early 1988 this same group helped us again with a grant to buy 15,000 Creole New Testaments.

Distributing these New Testaments has given real joy and contentment. Again and again I have watched faces light up as people eagerly begin to leaf through a New Testament. At times like that I wish every person who had given money for the printing and shipping of these New Testaments could stand beside me. It's a unique thrill to watch someone hold a New Testament for the first time in his life.

La Gonâve is a large island in the bay of Port-au-Prince. On that island we have a strong district of about 35 churches. Of the Nazarene pastors on La Gonâve Island, 18 of them recently completed an extension study program that gave them the education needed for ordination. During the four years of their studies, they met twice a month in a central mountain village for two days of classes.

On a trip out to La Gonâve to check the progress of that study group, I took several boxes of New Testaments. Getting to the village of Grand Source is never easy. First, you drive about an hour and a half up the coast from Port-au-Prince. There you have to wade out from a rocky beach and board an old wooden, leaky sailboat. Then you settle down for a two-hour ride to Anse-à-Galets on the coast of La Gonâve.

In that fishing village you'll find an ancient, battered Land Rover sitting under the shade of a lonely tree. You'll have to prayerfully coax the engine into starting, then nurse it along for about 45 minutes up a rocky mountain trail to Grand Source.

That particular afternoon when we arrived in Grand Source, the extension class was already under way. The pastors sat poring over their books. Eventually darkness forced the teacher to shut his notebook until morning. Along with the pastors, I walked up the hill in the front of the church. There ladies from the church were cooking supper for us. While we sat around waiting to eat, I got the boxes from the back of the Land Rover and divided the New Testaments among the pastors.

As I finished giving them out, the cooks showed up with plates piled high with rice and beans. I had about five or six New Testaments left over. I didn't know whether those ladies could read or not. I gave each of them a copy anyway. Thanking me profusely, they went back to work.

After the meal, we sat around talking and drinking strong, black Haitian coffee. Then the pastors drifted off into the darkness to their sleeping places. I had a small room in the little house where we had just eaten the evening meal. My room had an adequate bed. I knew it was perhaps the best bed in the whole village.

I felt drained that night. It had been a long, hard trip. Yet I had a hard time going to sleep. As I pulled the sheet over me, two of the cooks sat down at a small table not far from my window. One was a teenager. The other looked old enough to be her grandmother. Lighting a kerosene lamp, they brought out their new treasures, those Creole New Testaments.

The teenager was the more literate of the two. In the dim yellow light of that flickering oil lamp she began to read aloud. She stumbled along, the old woman watching her haltingly recognize the words one by one. The girl's voice was stuttering, uneven. Yet I detected a sense of awe as words from that New Testament leaped off the page at her.

Mixed emotions overcame me. A lump rose in my throat as I listened to those two reading aloud just outside my window. It was exciting. Yet I was also very tired. I yearned for sleep, but those voices outside my window kept me awake. Finally I drifted off to sleep listening to them read. Once those ladies had been blind. Now they were seeing. The Messiah had come. His kingdom was striking back.

One Sunday morning I heard rustling sounds in a village called Marlique. Not long after we arrived in Haiti, missionary John Burge gave out several boxes of New Testaments at Marlique. Our church there perches on a mountainside above Port-au-Prince, about a 20 to 30-minute drive from our Bible college campus. One Sunday I preached there. As I sat on the platform, looking over the crowd, I noticed people carrying New Testaments. They had received them in that earlier distribution effort.

Some of the covers of those paperback New Testaments had come off. A few of the copies even had a page or two of Matthew missing. The last chapter or so of Revelation was even gone from some of them. Nonetheless, those books were God's Word. His people had carried them to church to read together that morning.

As the service leader announced the Bible readings, I listened to that beautiful rustling sound of turning pages. The Lord had come. He was present in power and strength. He was marching with His troops against the enemy.

Sold Out

The first Protestant missionaries landed in Haiti over 100 years ago. Haitian Creole was not then a written language. The culturally prejudiced elite snootily regarded Creole as simply corrupted French. They thought teaching everyone to speak French properly would make Creole disappear. They were wrong. French and Creole certainly share a lot of vocabulary roots. Creole grammar, however, has little in common with French grammar. They are two completely different languages.

For many years the only Bible available in Haiti was in French. That's a language that even today only about 1 Haitian in 10 can readily understand. Even fluent French speakers use it as their second language. Their mother tongue is Creole. For even the most bilingual of Haitians, Creole remains the language of the heart and emotions.

By encouraging people to belittle Creole as merely badly spoken French, Satan kept a whole nation from having God's Word in their heart language. As long as people thought of Creole as just ineptly spoken French, it remained only an oral language. The devil was not to be successful, however. In the middle of this century, Protestant missionaries came up with a written form of Haitian Creole. Right away they set to work on Bible translation. In 1960 the first Haitian Creole version of the New Testament appeared.

A translating team went to work on the Old Testament. Satan was furious. The project met one fiendish obstacle after another. Once, a computer glitch erased the entire text.

Kingdom business can only be held back for so long, however. In early January 1986, news came that the first shipment of Creole Bibles was on its way from Asian printing plants. The day those Bibles arrived in Port-au-Prince's harbor, all the city was abuzz with the news. Pastors and laypeople flooded bookstores, trying to buy copies. Within four days the first printing of 55,000 sold out.

The Kingdom had struck back. Satan thought he could keep a nation in the dark. He was wrong. All across Haiti people are reading the Bible in their heart language. Praise the Lord!

As you pray for Haiti, thank the Lord that a promise is being fulfilled. That promise says: "Then the eyes of those who see will no longer be closed" (Isa. 32:3). Those who have been in physical darkness, spiritual darkness, and intellectual darkness are having their eyes opened. Truly the Messiah has come. We have seen the signs.

3

The Lepers Are Being Cured

David Livingstone. To many people his name is synonymous with missions—and for good reason. God used David Livingstone more than any other man to focus attention on Africa's appalling needs. Originally, Livingstone had dreamed of going to China. He wanted to go as a medical doctor. This interest in healing the sick once led him to write: "God had only one Son, and He gave Him to be a medical missionary."

That sentence highlights the importance of Jesus' healing ministry. While here on earth Jesus did spend a lot of time teaching and preaching. People called Him "Rabbi." That was a term reserved for respected teachers. He was, of course, much more than an outstanding teacher. He healed sick people! Those healing miracles were inextricably intertwined with His preaching and teaching. The Gospel accounts make them almost inseparable. You could even say that Jesus' total ministry was a healing one. It was a healing that sometimes was physical and other times spiritual.

The context in which Matthew places the Sermon on the Mount underscores this unity of the various facets of Jesus' ministry. Just before giving the text of that message, Matthew notes how Jesus healed "all who were ill with various diseases, those suffering severe pain, the demon-possessed, those having seizures, and the paralyzed" (4:24). After the text of the

message, Matthew tells how Jesus healed a leper and the
centurion's servant.

For His followers, Jesus modeled a ministry style aim
dealing with both physical and spiritual problems. Part
Kingdom's message is about our future destiny. It al
presses a burning concern for the quality of life in the he
now. Jesus modeled this concern for His followers. Th
went one step farther. He guided His close disciples t
hands-on experiences in resolving both physical and s
problems. For example, before He talked to John the
disciples about His Messiahship, Jesus had sent His
disciples on a preaching mission. In sending them, F
them authority to drive out evil spirits and to heal e
ease and sickness" (Matt. 10:1).

Another time "the Lord appointed seventy-two c
sent them two by two ahead of him to every town
where he was about to go" (Luke 10:1). Their task?
to have, like Him, a ministry of both preaching and f
told them: "When you enter a town . . . Heal the si
there and tell them, 'The kingdom of God is near
8-9). Here, as in His meeting with John's disciples,
lights the link between the Kingdom and healing

After Jesus' ascent to heaven, healing miracles
spicuous part of the apostles' ministries (Acts 5:1
Samarian revival led by Philip, for example, h
commonplace (8:5-8). Through the centuries, Jesu
the sick has set the tone. Following in their Mast
Christians have been known for their deep conce
and needy. Such compassion has shone most cl
cultural missionary thrusts.

The ministry of missionary medicine durir
years is the greatest humanitarian effort the
known. Where the gospel has gone, so has mee

ical missions, more than anything, disarms shrill critics of Christian missions. In Haiti today, for example, outside of Port-au-Prince Christians provide most health care. The Kingdom is striking back!

Across the cloud-capped mountains of Haiti and through its deep valleys, the Church of the Nazarene has planted churches. Nazarenes in Haiti have evangelized the lost. They have discipled believers. They have led them into the experience of heart holiness. There—where they work, witness, and evangelize—malaria and tuberculosis are widespread. Diarrhea, dysentery, scabies, tropical ulcers, and skin diseases are common. AIDS, venereal diseases, intestinal parasites, and typhoid fever take a heavy toll. When someone in an isolated village gets sick, God is often the only available doctor. The Church of the Nazarene has been working in Haiti for 40 years. Not surprisingly, through those years there have been ample testimonies of God's miraculous healing touch. Praise the Lord!

Alongside these miraculous displays stand those healings resulting from the ministry of medical personnel practicing the healing arts in Christ's name. In Haiti the Church of the Nazarene has an active medical ministry with qualified missionary and Haitian personnel.

The Witch Doctor Versus the Missionary

Bill Dawson, a physician's assistant and certified X-ray technician, has been a Nazarene missionary to Haiti since 1986. Once someone arrived asking him to make a house call not far from our main health center on the edge of Port-au-Prince. Normally patients living close to our health centers are asked to come in for treatment. This saves time and also means that the medical person has the diagnostic equipment of the clinic available to him.

On this day, however, they said the patient was too sick to move. So Bill grabbed his bag full of whatever medical people carry and took off.

When he arrived at the little house, he noticed coins scattered on the ground in front of the door. Startled, he stopped and looked around. He noticed other clear signs that a voodoo priest had been there before him. He knew they had called him as a last resort when the voodoo witch doctor's charms and spells had failed.

As he examined the sick man, Bill began to pray. The battle lines were clear: Voodoo had failed; Bill had come to bring healing in the name of Christ. Would he succeed? Bill treated the man and returned home. Then he called the other Nazarene missionaries and medical personnel to prayer. The tide of the disease turned, and the Lord got credit for a clear victory of healing.

The results aren't always that dramatic. Still, in Jesus' name, Nazarenes run healing ministries in Haiti and scores of other countries around the globe. The Messiah has come. He is at work in the world!

Nazarene concern with the physical well-being of Haitians goes back to the beginning of our work. Paul Orjala was the first Nazarene missionary to Haiti. Less than two years after his arrival he bought land near Port-au-Prince. It was to serve primarily as a Bible college campus.* At the entrance to the campus they also built a small dispensary.

*The site purchased near Port-au-Prince to be used as an educational campus has had several name changes throughout its history. References in this book to Nazarene Bible Insititute, Nazarene Bible School, Nazarene Bible College, and Haiti Nazarene Theological College refer to the same campus but reflect expanding educational purposes. Chapter 5 explains in more detail the latest program, TEE, Theological Education by Extension.

That original building has been enlarged three times. Missionary nurses like Lois Rodeheaver Ford, Carolyn Parsons, and Joan Reed worked there. Physician assistants Michelene Collins and Larry Wilson used it as a base for developing a Nazarene medical ministry in Haiti. Recent donations of equipment and supplies from U.S. hospitals and mission groups like REAP and Compassion International have turned the Nazarene Health Center into one of the best equipped in Haiti.

It provides low-cost medical care for the people nearby. It also is a training center and base of operations for a medical ministry seeking to touch all of Haiti. Nazarenes in Haiti run 24 rural pharmacy-dispensaries. Most of the health workers staffing these were trained in that main clinic near Port-au-Prince.

We now have a government-certified program that each year trains 6 to 12 village health workers. This means that each year 6 to 12 new villages will gain a qualified medical worker and a small but adequately stocked pharmacy. In addition, the medical staff there is working on an experimental project to try to ensure that every Nazarene church in Haiti has at least one person promoting good health, sanitation, and nutrition.

Jesus reminded John's disciples that, wherever He went, the sick were healed. Such a ministry continues around the world today.

The battle is not always easily won. Satanic forces have transformed some modern health care advances into frightful nightmares. To many Haitians, the hypodermic needle is the ultimate medical weapon. One injection carries more psychological weight than bottles of pills. A medical person's reputation often rests on how many shots he gives. Unprincipled charlatans have seized on this mistaken notion. With no medical training, they pose as medical experts. They offer to cure any ill with injections. In their greed they reuse unsterilized needles, spreading deadly diseases like AIDS and hepatitis.

Even those who escape serious complications often develop abscesses under the skin from dirty needles.

Nazarene medical missions provide a healing alternative to these quacks. Once again the Kingdom is counterattacking.

Why Not a Hospital?

People often ask: "Why don't Nazarenes build a hospital in Haiti?"

Good question. After all, Haiti needs more medical facilities. We Nazarenes have experience in running hospitals in India, Papua New Guinea, South Africa, and Swaziland. Why not Haiti?

There are good reasons for not building a Nazarene hospital in Haiti. It is not because we lack the money. It's not because we couldn't find committed people or that we lack the organizational know-how. Rather, we haven't built a hospital in Haiti because it does not fit our long-range goals.

The Gospels show that Jesus did not sit in one place, waiting for people to come to hear Him. His ministry was an itinerant one that combined healing and preaching everywhere He went. Matthew tells us that He "went through all the towns and villages, teaching in their synagogues, preaching the good news of the kingdom and healing every disease and sickness" (9:35). We're trying to follow a similar pattern. Our medical goal in Haiti is simple: health care for every village where the gospel of the Kingdom is preached. That's not original with us. Jesus showed us how.

Now, let's suppose the General Board had decided to build a hospital in Haiti. Hospitals gobble up money and personnel. Still, had we wanted to build a hospital in Haiti, I believe we could have done it. We would have found the money to build it and equip it. No doubt dedicated Nazarenes would have given their lives to staff it.

Here's the problem: We spend lots of money. We put together a top medical staff. But we would only be serving the health care needs of a small, limited area of Haiti. People in that one valley would have excellent medical care. That, however, would leave untouched all those other Haitian valleys where Nazarenes preach the gospel.

Our goal has been to meet health care needs wherever we're preaching the gospel. That's a lofty goal, given our limited resources. As Nazarene leaders have hammered out a workable strategy for Haiti, they've had to make choices. In medicine, we had two alternatives. The first alternative: Build a hospital and center our medical work in it. The second alternative: Develop a workable village-based health care program.

A strategy using community-based health care follows the advice given nearly 40 years ago by a Nazarene Commission on Medical Missions. This group gave its final report to the General Board in 1953. It concluded we could best reach our medical missions goals by focusing on small clinics and dispensaries. It cautioned against exhausting our limited resources in a few hospitals.

When this report came out, Nazarene work in Haiti was still in its early days. Noting that fact, the report gave some specific advice for Haiti. It proposed that we set up a dispensary at once in Haiti. It urged that mobile clinics become part of our Haitian medical ministry. That's the approach we've followed. From today's vantage point it has proven to be a wise course of action.

Where Nazarenes have gone preaching about the Messiah, we've also taken health care.

Community-Based Health Care
Not long ago I watched a red-and-white, four-wheel-drive Mitsubishi drive up on the Bible college campus. It parked in

front of the Nazarene Health Center. Purchased for our medical work by a Canadian government grant, that jeep was coming back from a rural trip. Dust covered every inch of it. The people getting out looked tired. A nurse, a tuberculosis agent, an M.D., and a couple of workers began unloading supplies and equipment. They had been out in an isolated valley on a two-day mobile clinic.

They were drained and wanted to get home. Still, they stopped briefly to tell me about their trip. As they talked, their faces began to light up. They had seen an unusual case or two. They glowed with excitement about the relief from suffering they had given. They were also pleased by the large number of people who had come for consultations.

A mobile clinic is a one- or two-day trip to an isolated village by our health center staff. It will have been announced in the church and community ahead of time. Thus, long before the Mitsubishi crammed with medical personnel and supplies appears around the last bend in the road, crowds will gather at the church.

Charges for seeing the doctor range from 20¢ in some areas to a high of $1.00. Patients also pay a small fee for medicine. These charges help offset the costs of this medical care; thus our resources stretch a bit farther. Charging something also keeps curiosity seekers from swamping the medical team with fictitious ailments. Of course, people with life-threatening problems get help even if they cannot pay the small fee.

Our dream is to assure a minimal level of health care in every outpost where there are Nazarenes. With over 300 churches already organized and new ones being planted every year, that's a faraway hope. Still, we're working at it.

One way will be through training what the Haitian government calls "health agents." We are working on government approval to train five or six of these at a time. Competent pastors and laymen will get five months of hands-on training in our main health center near Port-au-Prince. They'll then be qualified to open a small clinic and offer limited health care services.

The clinics will be an extension of the church's spiritual ministry. They mark the Church of the Nazarene as an organization that cares about people. They are signs of the Kingdom. Some of these men are planting brand-new churches in the areas where they open a dispensary. Thus medical missions is an integral part of the church planting and evangelism strategy for Haiti.

Nazarenes are preaching the gospel to the poor. The Lord is also using us to cleanse the lepers and heal all manner of other diseases. The Kingdom is striking back. And the Church of the Nazarene is part of it!

Immunization Program

Disease prevention is an important aspect of community health. One of public health's chief thrusts is inoculation against preventable killers and cripplers like polio, tetanus, diphtheria, and whooping cough. Immunizing people plays a key role in our medical ministry in Haiti.

Recently the Haitian government Health Ministry held a Polio Prevention Day, aimed at immunizing as many Haitian children as possible. Our clinic on the Bible college campus helped give those immunizations. Coincidentally, that day came during the Caribbean Regional Council meeting. Nazarene leaders from all over the Caribbean flew into Port-au-Prince. They met on the campus of Haiti Nazarene Bible College. Together they shared testimonies, looked at their shortcomings, and made plans for future outreach efforts in the Caribbean.

powerhouse that it provided one-fourth of the income of Napoleon's government.

Those glory days have vanished. Unfettered greed, the ravages of chronic civil strife, and havoc from natural and man-made ecological disasters have forced what used to be the "Pearl of the Antilles" to the brink of economic collapse. Over the past few decades, many million-dollar aid programs— American, United Nations, Canadian, German—have come to Haiti. Built on a misreading of human nature and blinded by cultural bias, most have been flushed down the drain of human greed.

To many it seems hopeless. Yet, in this forlorn picture, the preaching of the Kingdom has wrought powerful changes. In fact, the Church may be the only institution with enough courage, faith, and hope to face Haiti's appalling needs.

We know that the Kingdom's message is not "health and wealth." That kind of message grows out of materialism and appeals primarily to carnal self-centeredness, breeding smug complacency in the face of our world's crying needs. A "God wants you rich" message cannot transform palsied limbs. What can bring wholeness to financially crippled people in places like Haiti will be compassionate love coupled with inner changes brought about by the Holy Spirit.

When someone surrenders his life to enter the Kingdom, the Holy Spirit begins to help rearrange priorities. Vices sponging up precious money are abandoned. Gambling at cockfights, drinking rum, and buying and selling sexual favors are not part of Kingdom living. Some of these changes in life-style following conversion cause what sociologists call "redemption lift."

Redemption lift is the upward economic and social mobility experienced by many Christians. After turning to Christ, people often become more productive. Born-again believers no longer squander their resources as they did before conversion. As a result, despair can become hope, and people can begin to inch up the economic ladder. Since Haiti's per capita gross national product totals less than $400 annually, that climb may not seem very far to us. It is there, nonetheless, and it is upward.

The unique emphases of holiness groups like the Church of the Nazarene are important aspects here. Heb. 12:14 is a classic holiness text. We Nazarenes know this verse. We often quote it from memory: "Follow peace with all men, and holiness, without which no man shall see the Lord" (KJV).

Recently I took time to study the context of this well-known verse. The verse immediately before speaks of "the lame [who need] not be disabled, but rather healed." Healing and holiness appear together in the same paragraph!

As holiness people, we are glad to be part of helping make a difference in Haiti. While the gospel makes no ironclad promises of an improved financial picture, a better life is sometimes a positive by-product of changes taking place when men and women yield themselves totally to God.

Funds coming from Nazarenes around the world are helping get economic cripples up and walking. One of the programs run by the office of Nazarene Compassionate Ministries is called Venture Capital Development. This is not General Budget money. Rather, these are gifts over and above the basic lifeline support of General Budget. Such Venture Capital money funds social transformation projects. These range from organizing hog raising cooperatives to helping pastors' wives set up small market stalls.

Oink, Oink

Haiti's economic base is primarily agricultural. Most Haitians are subsistence farmers, eking out a living on one rocky acre or less. High population density, poor farming practices, and lack of money have combined to make Haiti a net importer of foodstuffs.

As we have worked to develop mature, self-supporting churches and districts in Haiti, it has only been natural that we would be involved in farming projects. During the 1960s and 1970s, Haiti's missionary force included agronomists Charles Morrow and Elvin DeVore. At present there are no Nazarene agmissionaries in Haiti. We are, however, still involved in farming projects.

Some of the most visible and productive of these projects are district-run pig breeding projects. One of the main goals of our pig projects is to provide rural pastors with a pair of pigs: a male and a female. From this start, the pastor will have a supply of meat. He will also get cash income from the sale of piglets. Thus our pig projects help pastors develop a stable economic support base for themselves and their families.

The oldest of these pig projects is at Jacmel, an old pirate haven nestled in a cove on the south coast. Another pig project has been in operation for some time at Les Étroits on the island of La Gonâve. Four more projects are in various beginning stages.

The South District pig project began with a grant from Nazarene Compassionate Ministries. The La Gonâve pig project began with profits from another economic aid project, a small wholesale/retail business. Earlier, Nazarene Compassionate Ministries had provided start-up capital for this store.

Start-up capital for a pig project builds shelters for the pigs. It constructs cisterns to catch and hold rainwater. It buys initial stocks of food. It builds dry, secure storage areas to hold these feeding supplies. Top-quality sows and boars are bought from the government agriculture ministry.

As little piglets come along, they are given to pastors who also receive training on raising and breeding them. A pastor's responsibility to the district often includes giving back one piglet from his first litter. After it got started, the project near Jacmel expanded to include goats. Recently, district leaders also began raising mules. These are given to pastors to use for traveling in rugged mountain areas.

Economic cripples are rising to their feet. The Messiah has come.

Eggplants in the Churchyard

Dismayed, I gazed one day down into a big burlap sack. It was full of eggplants—big, shiny, purple eggplants. I looked up into the face of the pastor who had handed me the sack. He grinned from ear to ear. It was a gift to me, he said, from his church at Mar Joeffrey. My heart sank. I don't like eggplants. But there they were, a whole sack of them.

I couldn't refuse them. To bring me that burlap sack, this pastor had ridden five hours in the back of an old, rickety, gaily painted truck. So I thanked him profusely for his thoughtfulness.

The story began several months earlier. The pastor, Rev. Jenel Gabriel, was a student in one of my extension classes. He invited me to visit his church. It's out near the Dominican Republic border. So one Saturday afternoon I made that dusty, rocky drive to Mar Joeffrey to be a part of the Sunday morning service. After that service, the children of the church took me out to see their farm project. Back of their tin-roofed, pole church building lay several raised vegetable beds. Those neatly made beds were chock full of tiny tomato and eggplant seedlings.

I oohed and ahed over the seedbeds. Then I made everyone line up behind one of the beds for a photo like those that sometimes appear in furlough slide shows. Rev. Gabriel explained that the little plants go to families in the rural community. The project was a program of the local Nazarene school. The schoolkids had gone through that dirt and sifted out all the stones. They'd tilled in organic matter. Every day they carried vessels filled with water on their heads to sprinkle over the seedlings.

They told me that a government agronomist was helping them. Stationed just a few miles away, he came by once a week to check the seedling project. During his visits, he spent time teaching the children how to improve their yields.

After lunch that Sunday afternoon I returned home to Port-au-Prince. Months went by. In little gardens all over that village those tiny eggplant seedlings grew and blossomed and bore fruit. The people remembered my interest in the project. So they sent me a sack of that purple fruit. I was grateful for their thoughtfulness, but not for the eggplants. If I remember correctly, we gave them to needy families who happened to like eggplants.

Producing more food means that the lame start taking some steps forward. The Kingdom is striking back.

Another Nazarene aid project was sewing cooperatives. We imported about 100 used foot-powered sewing machines and distributed them in several of our churches. An initial stock of cloth went along with each sewing machine. A Nazarene woodcraft shop also operated for several years in Port-au-Prince. Men who learned their craft in this shop now produce things for sale to tourists.

There have been other ventures, like a dry-cleaning business. We financed rural bus transportation and even casket making. Some of our experimental crash projects crashed badly. Others continue to provide needed incomes for pastors and laypeople. Even those that failed taught us some things.

Lessons learned in these failures have helped other projects succeed. The result is that economic cripples begin to walk. Outside aid money combined with redemption lift is making a difference in the lives of believers. When enough individuals change, so do their communities.

There's a Highway There, and a Way

Local churches sometimes take leadership in organizing the people of a rural village into a force for development. For instance, in several villages Nazarenes have formed themselves into road-building brigades. Using picks and shovels, they carve out roads to their mountain villages.

Having a road into a village makes it easier to convince the government to provide health and education services to that area. It's also easier for the village to get farm products to market. A happy by-product is that a road makes it easier to get in building supplies for homes, churches, and schools. Occasionally, Approved Special money arrives to buy picks and shovels. We've used that to help these road-building cooperatives buy shovels and sometimes even a wheelbarrow. Nazarene-led road projects in Boy Roi and Madame Julien have benefited from this kind of Approved Special gifts.

These roads are quite crude. You still need a four-wheel-drive vehicle to get over them. However, if the Kingdom had not invaded those villages, these roads would not be there. The Holy Spirit draws men into the Church. There they bond into loving, caring communities. These churches become natural focal points for community action projects. Leadership gifts discovered and developed in the church are put to use for the good of the whole community. The Kingdom is thus striking back. The lame are beginning to walk—and they're getting better roads on which to do it.

Flash Flood!

On October 19, 1986, a flash flood hit parts of the island of La Gonâve. Torrents of water went rushing down mountain gullies, smashing into villages on the seashore. The flood ravaged two towns with Nazarene churches, Anse-à-Galets and Trou Jacques. Among the dead and missing were 19 Nazarenes. Some bodies swept out to sea were never recovered.

By the next day Nazarene relief was on its way. We loaded a truck with sacks of rice and beans from our warehouse near Port-au-Prince and sent it down to our boat dock. There the sacks of food supplies left for La Gonâve on little sailboat ferries. Nazarene Hunger and Disaster funds helped resettle families who had lost their homes. In Trou Jacques the village decided to leave their narrow canyon and move up on a hill. We helped the church purchase a large enough piece of property so that most of the affected Nazarene families would have room to build their new homes.

We were also able to send several boxes of used clothing left earlier by people on Work and Witness teams. Having this clothing on hand was providential. Restrictive tariffs and stiff regulations try to protect jobs in Haiti's small clothing industry. So it is difficult to ship used clothing to Haiti. However, Nazarene visitors to Haiti often empty their suitcases before leaving. The only clothes many work team members take home are what they are wearing. Their generosity gives us supplies of used clothing for emergencies such as this flood.

The food, clothing, and shelter we were able to provide helped those crippled by the flash flood to begin walking again.

On June 23, 1987, another flash flood struck the church and parsonage at Goyard. The pastor's garden and his pigs were swept away. He and his family lost all their personal effects. The next day, word of the tragedy reached District Superintendent Rev. Lumanite Costume. He got on his motorcycle to see firsthand what had happened.

Then he headed for Port-au-Prince to enlist the missionaries' help in requesting relief help from Nazarene Compassionate Ministries. By Friday, just two days after the flood, aid from the Nazarene Hunger and Disaster Fund was on its way. Once again, used clothing left by Work and Witness team members helped a family replace what they had lost.

The Kingdom intervened once more. The Messiah has come!

Insurance policies sometimes refer to disasters like these flash floods as "acts of God." What a travesty on words!

Visitors to Haiti often remark that its mountains are barren. Their scarred faces lie exposed to the blazing sun and the torrential downpours of the rainy season. In past years greedy men systematically and ruthlessly denuded Haiti's forested mountains. Once-lush mahogany forests were stripped away. No trees were replanted. Today the few trees that survived the logging industry come down to make charcoal for cooking fires. I've even seen people digging up tree roots to make charcoal.

When heavy rains fall on these mountains, devastating flash floods are inevitable. It is man—not God—who bears the final responsibility for such "natural" disasters.

God's kingly rule in the lives of believers works to lessen and relieve the tragic results of such events. Nevertheless, they are painful times, and the church does what it can to ease suffering and pain. Such tragedies do not mean evil is winning. What we see are only evidences of evil's thrashing death agony. In the end the kingdom of darkness is going to lose. Even today its power is being challenged. The kingdom of God has struck back. People crippled by natural disasters are beginning to walk again.

Want to Plant a Tree?

One predictable result of heavy deforestation is the washing away of topsoil from mountainous slopes. All you can see on many slopes where people have their gardens are rocks and stones. Not a cupful of topsoil can be seen. Still, at planting time people will be there digging holes with machetes to plant corn and beans.

A second tragic result of deforestation is that rainwater runs off the stony slopes. It does not percolate slowly into the ground as it would if there were heavy tree cover. As a result, water tables have dropped. Small spring-fed mountain streams have dried up, further complicating the lives of subsistence farmers.

The Church of the Nazarene is trying to change this by encouraging reforestation. Years ago, when Paul Orjala bought that hill near Port-au-Prince for a Bible college campus, it was barren. Today thousands of trees cover those 29 acres. We bought some of those trees; the government forest service provided others. Many of the newest ones came from our health center custodian. He collects seeds from mature trees on campus. He plants those seeds in little plastic sacks filled with dirt, then he waters them carefully. When they sprout, he cares for them until they can be transplanted somewhere on the campus. We also give away little trees from his nursery to pastors and patients at the health center.

It will, of course, take millions—probably billions—of trees to reforest Haiti. Still, regardless of the astronomical numbers involved, those trees must be planted one at a time. So we're trying to do our part. I even like to encourage tourists to plant at least one tree while they are in Haiti.

Madame Artaud called me one day. An elite Haitian who lives next to our campus, she works in all kinds of neighborhood action projects. This time she was calling about a tree planting project. The government forest service and the Roman Catholic church were cosponsoring a "bless the tree" day. Most of the Roman Catholic churches in Port-au-Prince were going to give out small trees to all worshipers on the following Sunday. She wanted to know if the Church of the Nazarene would like to participate.

I told her we probably would. I said we probably would not "bless" the trees like the Roman Catholic priests would be doing. I told her, however, that Nazarenes liked to plant trees. We would also fervently pray that God would use the efforts to bring healing to the land. She asked how many trees I thought we could use.

"Two hundred," I said.

"Not enough," she responded. "You need to take at least 1,000."

I gulped and said OK. Time was short. It was already the middle of the week. However, all 10 of the area Nazarene churches that I contacted were eager to take part.

On Saturday afternoon, we took a jeep and a pickup to the distribution point. It took us more than one trip to get all 1,000 trees in their little dirt-filled, plastic bags. That evening we were busy until ten o'clock delivering them to the churches. The next morning at the end of church services in and around Port-au-Prince, 1,000 Nazarene families got a free tree. They promised to plant that tree near their house. They agreed to water it and keep animals and people from trampling it.

One of the Nazarene churches receiving trees was Marlique, that mountain church above Port-au-Prince where we had also distributed some Bibles. Late Saturday night up that rocky, gravel road I went. The back of our jeep was crammed with 75 trees.

On Tuesday my telephone rang. It was Pierre Walliere, the pastor from Marlique. His church had planted all 75 of their trees. That had whetted their appetites. Now they wanted to start to work on the whole mountainside. Pierre wanted to know if I could get them *3,000* more seedlings. I gulped a bit and said I'd try.

I went to see Madame Artaud, the lady who'd arranged for us to get the original 1,000. A couple of days later she called me back. The government forest service had agreed to provide Marlique Nazarenes with 3,000 free trees. Moreover, along with ordinary forest-type trees, they agreed to provide some fruit- and nut-bearing trees. They also offered to help oversee the project to assure a maximum survival rate of the seedlings.

After the trees were planted, government agronomists made an inspection trip to Marlique. Impressed with the way church members were caring for the new little trees, they gave them another 15,000 trees. They also helped organize students from a nearby government high school to go up the mountain to help the Nazarenes plant these 15,000 trees.

Now the Marlique Nazarenes are working with the government forestry people, perfecting a long-range plan for their mountain. They want to plant 1 *million* trees. Seventy-five scraggly-looking seedlings in tiny black plastic sacks had started something that will revolutionize a mountain.

Vocational Schools

The Church of the Nazarene is helping the lame and crippled to walk again in many ways. Dr. Steve Weber spent two terms as a missionary to Haiti. Today he heads the office of Nazarene Compassionate Ministries. Steve is fond of quoting the Chinese proverb: "Give a man a fish, and you feed him today. Give him a hook, teach him to fish, and you feed him forever." One of the ways we are helping the lame and crippled walk again is by teaching people new skills they can use to earn a living.

Putting bread in front of hungry people helps them. It keeps them alive. Equipping people with trade skills goes beyond this. It gives them the bakery in which they can make their own bread. Setting up vocational schools seems a wise investment of aid money.

Two of our districts are now running vocational schools. One opened in 1986 on the south coast in a town named Jacmel. An evening program teaches cooking, sewing, and typing to girls from that area. The school also has intensive courses that go all day, five days a week. Girls from churches all over the district come in for a month at a time to learn trade skills in these intensive courses.

In the fall of 1987 another Nazarene vocational school opened in Port-de-Paix up on the northern coast. This school offers courses in welding and carpentry besides the home economics and secretarial skills taught at Jacmel. Both schools got started with grants from Nazarene Compassionate Ministries.

There are also many initiatives being taken by local churches. For instance, our Grand Source church runs sewing courses. Our Pétionville church in suburban Port-au-Prince has organized courses for hopeful electricians. In downtown Port-au-Prince the Bel Air Church uses donated treadle sewing machines to train seamstresses. Our Marlique church uses donated manual typewriters to run a typing school. One of our rural pastors on the northwest peninsula, Rev. Delius Ambeau, teaches straw weaving to his members. Scott Hannay first came to Haiti on specialized assignment to teach welding and auto mechanics at the mission garage. Today, one of his first students is the mission mechanic.

The lame are learning to walk. The Kingdom is striking back.

General Budget?

As economic cripples begin to walk, they discover the joy of participating in the church's global outreach. At the 1987 Caribbean Regional Conference, all the districts of the Caribbean voted to accept General Budget shares for each of their churches. For some this was a new step. For the Haitians it was old hat. Haitian Nazarenes may be among the poorest people of the world. Still, for years they have given General Budget offerings.

At Easter time one year I listened to Rev. Lorius Dessources exhorting his people on La Gonâve.

"If you want a nickel blessing," he said, "put a nickel in your envelope. If, on the other hand, you want a 50-cent blessing, put 50 cents in!"

Haitian Nazarenes receive a lot of missions dollars. They are also on the giving end. Economic cripples who are starting to walk are now helping pass healing along to others. Praise the Lord!

5

The Deaf Are Hearing

Ears are important to Kingdom people. I remember watching Bill Dawson poke something into a little boy's ear. It looked like a flashlight with a tiny funnel on one end. Bill, a Nazarene medical missionary, told me it was an otoscope. He said he could even look up my nose with it.

He peered intently through the little funnel into the boy's ear. Turning to me, he rattled off some impressive-sounding medical terms. Seeing I looked puzzled, he hugged the little Haitian while he explained to me that a fungus was growing in the boy's ear. That sounded awful. Bill, however, assured me it wasn't serious. He told the parents how to use vinegar to clear up the problem.

Ears. Scripture talks a lot about them and our sense of hearing. The Bible says that God has revealed himself to man. We have five senses: sight, touch, taste, smell, and hearing. In revealing himself to us, He often uses that last one, our sense of hearing. The letters to the seven churches in Revelation 2—3 all end with the stringent demand: "He who has an ear, let him hear what the Spirit says to the churches."

In the Old Testament priestly consecration ceremony the priests had sacrificial blood smeared on their ears, a sign of obedience in spiritual hearing (Exod. 29:20). The ears of cleansed lepers were also to be touched with blood. Jesus called the ears of the disciples "blessed" because they heard "the secrets of the kingdom of heaven" (Matt. 13:16, 11). Against this background, it should not be surprising to discover Messianic prophecies dealing with ears and hearing.

Isaiah prophesied: "In that day the deaf will hear the words of the scroll" (29:18). The last of Job's "comforters," Elihu, tells him that God uses affliction to open a humble man's ears so that he will listen to God's inward voice (36:15). When John's disciples came asking about Jesus' Messiahship, it naturally followed that Jesus would point out to them that deaf ears were being unstopped.

As God works through the Church of the Nazarene in places like Haiti, deaf people regain their hearing. Believers testify occasionally to miraculous healings coming as the result of prayer. These have come without any human instrumentality. There are also those healings coming as God guides the hands of skilled Nazarene medical personnel.

In at least one instance God has used a talented Nazarene construction contractor to thwart the disabling effects of physical deafness. Evidence of that lies on the main highway north out of Port-au-Prince. There, on the east side of the highway, are several one-story white buildings. There's no sign out front. Everyone knows, however, that it's the evangelical school for deaf children.

For a few years, Freddy Williams supervised Nazarene construction projects in Haiti. While there he built a lot of Nazarene churches. He also gave his expertise to build most of the buildings at the deaf school. Because of his help, deaf children are becoming functioning members of Haitian society. Few of these children will experience miraculous, immediate opening of their ears. Few of them will benefit from high-tech medical and surgical advances used in developed countries. Yet, because of caring Christians—including a Nazarene builder—the devastating results of their deafness are being blunted. To me that's another clear sign of the Kingdom's inauguration.

"How Shall They Hear Without a Preacher?"

Among all the parts of the human body, the ear may be the most important as we contemplate fulfilling the Great Commission. The seeming "foolishness of preaching" (1 Cor. 1:21, KJV) is the way the gospel message reaches most people. That's true even in our day of the printed page and video image. Even the written Word often reaches our hearts as other people read it aloud to us. Interwoven into sermons and testimonies, the written Word comes alive as the spoken Word. Day and night, around the globe, the gospel of the Kingdom continues to be proclaimed by human voices and received by human ears.

One inescapable conclusion is that there must be someone to proclaim it. Restoring hearing to a physically deaf person is a marvelous thing. Even then, the good news of the Kingdom will not be good news for him unless messengers proclaim that message in his hearing. In Rom. 10:14 Paul comes to this same conclusion. He asks: "How shall they hear without a preacher?" (KJV). One must hear the gospel before he can either receive it reject it. One of the ways the Church of the Nazarene helps spiritually deaf Haitians is by training Spirit-filled leaders to preach and teach the good news of the Kingdom.

Nazarenes began work in Haiti 40 years ago. Right from the start we poured General Budget dollars into training Haitian pastors and evangelists. When Paul Orjala arrived in Haiti in 1950, one of his top priorities was training national leaders. Not many months after stepping off the airplane, he had begun an evening school for prospective pastors. As I mentioned earlier, as soon as the Lord provided money, he bought land near the capital city and began construction of Bible school classrooms and dormitories. Through the years, graduates of this school have helped fill that void for preachers that the apostle Paul lamented.

Men trained in the Bible school and its related extension programs not only are today leading Nazarene congregations in Haiti but also are pastoring churches of Haitian immigrants in the United States, Canada, the Bahamas, and France.

Today, Nazarene General Budget money finances three different types of training programs for Haitian pastors and evangelists. The most visible of these is a traditional Bible college near Port-au-Prince. It has dormitories, classrooms, and a dining hall. In this campus setting, young Haitian men spend four years studying for the ministry. On the weekends they get practical ministry experience. Under Dr. Jeanine Van Beek's guidance entrance requirements for this school were gradually raised. Today they include the equivalent of a U.S. high school diploma.

The second type of program is called Pastoral Extension Training. This decentralized theological education has men studying in several locations throughout Haiti. Most of these men are married and have children. All are already pastoring churches. A recent study showed that men entering the extension programs have pastored for an average of seven years when they begin their studies. All are bivocational. That means the local church is not their only source of income. On alternate weeks they meet in a central location for two days of classes. Thus they continue pastoring their churches and providing for their families while studying toward ordination.

Besides these two programs receiving General Budget subsidies, there is a third type of church leadership training. It is even more decentralized. Furthermore, it requires no outside funding. This is the training given local leaders by pastors themselves. Often informal and unstructured, it is, nonetheless, effective training.

Many churches hold Saturday afternoon classes for Sunday School teachers. There they go over the lesson for Sunday, discussing the main points of the lesson and ways to teach that particular lesson. Some churches will not allow a teacher who misses a Saturday training session to teach the next morning.

Most local churches have several local preachers. These men and women preach or exhort in open-air meetings and in weekly services at preaching points. Often they are the evangelists in revival meetings in the home church. All this is done under the watchful eye of the veteran pastors.

This on-the-job training produces leaders for the church planting efforts we call "stations." Most of our rural pastors come from this large pool of experienced preachers. Once a man has charge of an organized local church, he can enter our extension study program. There he will get the formal training required for ordination. The church in Haiti has had tremendous growth. Allowing leaders to emerge in the local church and make their way into the pastorate has assured us a surplus of good preachers.

Three types of training: college campus, extension centers, and local church. Their graduates provide ample evidence that the Messiah has come. Through these trained leaders those who once seemed deaf to the Good News are beginning to hear it clearly.

A Cross, a Bible, and a Dove

Visitors to the campus of Haiti Nazarene Theological College usually park in front of a stylized cross, dove, and open Bible. These symbols are part of a wrought-iron grillwork enclosing an open area of the student lounge. Craig Zickefoose spent two years in Haiti on a specialized assignment. While there he made that grillwork. He used the three symbols to represent the college's goals: to ground students in the Word (the open Bible) as they prepare to preach the crucified and resurrected Christ (the cross) in the power of the Holy Spirit (the dove).

Nazarene Theological College sits on a 29-acre campus above Port-au-Prince. Approximately 45 students follow a study program similar to that at Nazarene Bible College in Colorado Springs. Each year, about three times more young men apply than the school can handle. Those wishing to enter must take an entrance exam and have an interview with one of the college professors. The most qualified are accepted as students.

The students are all Haitian. The school, however, has a distinct global flavor. Jeanine Van Beek, the former director, was Dutch and spoke at least five languages. There are Haitian professors like Remy Cherenfant, Marcel Sainvilus, and Charles Dumerzier. Nazarene missionaries teaching on the staff have come from the United States, Canada, and Great Britain. Together, this international team assures that the message preached to listening ears is clear and uncompromising. The Church of the Nazarene is a global church. Haiti Nazarene Theological College makes that clear!

Nazarene Theological College has one of the best French-language theological libraries in Haiti. It seeks to maintain studies on a high academic level. Of primary concern, however, is the spiritual tone of the students. For four years we lived on the edge of the campus. On many mornings we were awakened at 6 A.M. by music from the school chapel as students began their day with singing and a prayer meeting. There are also twice-weekly chapel services. Thursday morning is prayer and fasting time. No breakfast is served. Classes start an hour later than usual.

From time to time revival tides sweep across the campus. I remember Trevor Johnston telling of a doctrine of holiness class that turned into an altar service.

The Messiah has come. The deaf are hearing.

An Army Without Weapons

"We were pastoring churches. We were, however, like soldiers trying to fight a war without any guns. Now we've got those weapons we needed."

With this little flourish, Louis Florestin finished his speech. A chorus of nine loud "Amens" followed. The speech marked the end of four years of extension studies for 10 veteran pastors. On their final day of classes they asked me to be present. They wanted to say, "Thank you," to the church for providing training for them.

They were waiting for me in the classroom when I arrived. The other nine pushed Louis Florestin forward. He delivered his impromptu speech to an audience of one (me) as the rest of the pastors stood behind him, beaming.

Louis' story began a few years earlier in the large Gonaïves church. He was converted there as a young man. Soon some leadership potential began showing through. His formal education had ended in elementary school. It became clear rather early, however, that the Holy Spirit had endowed him with the gift of preaching.

Louis' pastor, who was also a district superintendent, urged him to listen carefully to the Lord. In Louis, Rev. Duroc Placide thought he saw signs of God's call to the pastoral ministry. Not long afterward, Rev. Placide asked Louis to become pastor of the Chevreau Lombard church.

Chevreau Lombard lies in the fertile Artibonite Valley, surrounded by rice paddies. Our church there is fairly new. At that time it was muddling along, leaderless. Seeking a better financial future for himself and his family, the previous pastor had left abruptly for France.

Louis' only training for the ministry was some on-the-job training in preaching and group leadership dynamics. Still, he prayed through, accepted the challenge, and moved with his family to Chevreau Lombard. Very soon he came to feel he had gone to war without any weapons. What was he to do? He had only an elementary school education, so he could not get into Haiti's Nazarene Theological College. Even if he had been qualified, he wasn't sure he wanted to leave the active ministry for four years.

Then came the announcement that an extension program for untrained pastors was being started. Louis elbowed his way to the front of the line to enroll. He was accepted and began making trips to Port-au-Prince every two weeks to meet with fellow pastors for classes.

Now, four years later, he had finished the course of study. At the next district assembly he would be eligible for ordination. More importantly for him, he felt that now he had those weapons he needed. The other pastors in that group asked him to be their spokesperson in expressing their thanks.

Louis and his nine fellow workers were in our Pastoral Extension Training program. PET is nontraditional ministerial training. It's more commonly called Theological Education by Extension. Aimed at students who already have families and jobs, TEE offers education in a nondisruptive format. TEE allows a student to continue his productive relation to society. It does not uproot a person, forcing him to move to a campus.

Such ministerial training parallels John Wesley's training program for lay preachers. We also have something similar in the U.S. From our beginning days under Bresee, we've had a home Course of Study. Men unable to go to a college or seminary use the home Course of Study method under the direction of veteran pastors on their district. Our PET program in Haiti can be viewed as a development of that concept.

Since we entered Haiti, we've tried several kinds of nonresident study programs for pastors. None of them, however, were designed to fulfill *Manual* requirements for ordination. As a result, until recently a person being considered for ordination in Haiti had to have graduated from the resident Bible college. Thus we had a lot of successful pastors like Louis Florestin who were locked out of ordination.

Requiring Bible college training can be a formidable barrier to ordination in countries like Haiti. It doesn't really square with what Nazarenes believe about the call to the ministry and the church's recognition of that call. We don't believe God looks for a diploma before He calls a man to preach. So, in 1981 Dr. Jeanine Van Beek and Dr. Steve Weber launched a program to bring the Haitian districts more in line with Nazarene beliefs and practices regarding the ministry.

Their Pastoral Extension Training was modeled on programs successfully used elsewhere bearing the label Theological Education by Extension. The design, however, that Dr. Van Beek and Dr. Weber came up with has some unique things about it. First, before a person can apply for entrance, he must *already* be pastoring. Feeling a call to the ministry is not enough to get in; the students in this program must be in the active pastoral ministry.

One of the reasons for this rule was the large numbers of veteran pastors without formal training. When our PET program began, we had 150 unordained pastors in Haiti. We wanted to train these men first, since they were already pastoring.

Such a rule also ensures that the students share a common characteristic. Our extension students vary widely in their ages. Some have only a third grade education; a few have university training. Their ability to do individualized study varies. All, however, face similar problems each week as they pastor churches. Whatever their other differences, this shared characteristic bonds them together.

A second unique characteristic of our program is that once a group starts classes, it stays together for the entire four years of the program. After the first year, no new students are allowed to join a group. Therefore, although these men do not live together on a campus, they still spend two days together twice a month over a four-year period. Thus group dynamics get a chance to form and develop.

This extension program is making a difference in the ministries of the Haitian Nazarene pastors. At any one time we have about 65 men in various groups. This program is helping the church respond to the question: "How shall they hear without a preacher?" The Kingdom is striking back. Those pastors are being trained and sent out.

Some time ago I was out on the island of La Gonâve, checking the progress of our extension group there. In the evening I sat talking with the district superintendent. He began telling me about the positive impact the program was having on the lives of some of the pastors. Sometimes the changes in ministry had been dramatic.

He mentioned one pastor who had been around for several years. Unfortunately, his church had stagnated. It was not growing. It didn't even have very many signs of spiritual life.

The district superintendent enrolled that pastor in the extension study program. There he began to study the Bible, theology, church history, how to conduct a worship service, and how to lead a congregation. After some months the district superintendent visited his church. He could hardly believe his eyes. Those extension studies were revolutionizing that man's preaching and pastoral leadership. His church was responding. It had come alive and begun to grow.

Not long ago a handwritten note arrived from the Michaud church board. This church, located on the road from Port-au-Prince to the Dominican Republic, was seeing some positive changes in their pastor since he entered our extension study program. Under their pastor's revitalized guidance they were finding new spiritual strength and seeing progress in their church. So they wrote a note expressing their appreciation to the general church for sponsoring the extension study program.

How shall they hear without a preacher? They won't. That's why ministerial training programs are so important. Because of such programs, previously deaf Haitian ears now hear.

Again and again I have been awed by the Haitian pastors' appetite for learning. Every two weeks some walk as much as six hours one way to get to their study center. One man on La Gonâve has to start walking the day before classes. He sleeps under a tree beside the path and gets up early the next morning to finish walking. When these pastors are at the center, they may have to sleep on a rough church pew. Amazingly, I rarely heard complaints about the physical discomforts and sacrifices they made to participate in the extension program.

As we started our first group on La Gonâve, I tried to hold enrollment to a maximum of 12 students. A smaller class size enables the professor to give students personalized attention. It also allows for more class participation by each individual. I also knew it would be easier to find sleeping places for a limited group of pastors.

At that time we only had 3 ordained pastors among the 30 serving on La Gonâve. All 27 of the others wanted to be in that first group. District Superintendent Lorius Dessources helped narrow down the list of applicants to 12 men. We sent word to those 12 that they had been accepted.

On the first day of classes, those 12 men showed up. So did 6 other pastors. I patiently explained that only those officially enrolled could participate in the program. I explained why we wanted to limit class size. I tried to explain our problems with feeding and housing more than a dozen. Solemnly they all nodded. I thought they understood.

Two weeks later the class met again. This time *eight* extra men showed up. Again I tried to convince them there would eventually be places in a class for everyone. They needed to be patient, to wait their turn.

I finally got through to everyone—except Fils Garilomme. He kept coming. He knew he wasn't in the class. He couldn't sit with those that were enrolled. So he would wait outside until the class session got under way in the back corner of the sanctuary. Then he would slip in the side door opening off the platform. Sitting up on one of the front pews, he would strain intently, trying to hear what was said in the back of the church. He even brought along a notebook and painstakingly took notes.

I talked to him in private. I told him we did not have enough food to feed him. "No problem," he said.

I told him I wasn't sure we could find a place for him to sleep. "No problem," he said. Sure enough, in the evenings he just disappeared. To this day I have no idea where he slept. Before long, at mealtimes I noticed that everyone in the group was taking a little less. They had apparently convinced the cooks to slip a plate out back to Rev. Garilomme.

I marveled at this young man. Every two weeks he was willing to walk several hours even though I held out no hope of his getting credit for the classes. "No problem," he said. He just wanted to learn how to be a better pastor. After nearly a year, the Lord started talking to me about Rev. Garilomme. I relented and let him enroll in the class.

When I started going to La Gonâve for this extension group, I thought I would be the teacher. I became a student instead. Fils Garilomme taught me a lot of things. An unwavering determination to fulfill his divine calling drove him to turn obstacles into stepping-stones. He cared deeply for his people. His love for them drove him to learn how to pastor. Men like him are clear evidence that the Kingdom has come. Their willingness to pay any price, to make any sacrifice to preach the gospel, guarantees that the deaf world will hear the Good News.

Sanctified, Spirit-filled Haitians like Rev. Garilomme are being prepared to proclaim the good news of the Kingdom to those newly unstopped ears. Fils Garilomme is a sign that the Messiah is at work.

Missionary Training Ground

While we've been training pastors and evangelists in Haiti, another kind of school has also been operating. Haiti has been a school for many Nazarene missionaries filling key positions in our global outreach. Among these was pioneer missionary Paul Orjala. After three terms in Haiti Paul Orjala left to become Nazarene Theological Seminary's first professor of missions. Dr. Orjala accomplished a lot during his 14 years in Haiti. He also learned a lot of things. The lessons he learned in Haiti were used to train young people now serving as Nazarene missionaries.

Walter and Linda Crow got their start in Haiti. From there they went to open the work in France. After getting that work started, Walt spent five years as president of European Nazarene Bible College.

Harry Rich, current district superintendent in French-speaking Quebec, began his cross-cultural career in Haiti.

Terry Read was one of Dr. Paul Orjala's students at seminary. Terry began his missionary career in Haiti. After two terms there he transferred to Brazil. Recently he went to Kansas City to teach missions at the seminary. He's filling the vacancy originally left by Paul Orjala when he went to France in 1987.

Steve Weber now directs Nazarene Compassionate Ministries. Working out of the World Mission Division office in Kansas City, he oversees Nazarene involvement with primary and secondary education, medical work, disaster relief, and economic development. He helps channel Nazarene responses to needs in countries where we don't yet have churches. Before going to Kansas City, Steve and Linda Weber were missionaries to Haiti. Before that he, too, had studied at seminary under Paul Orjala.

Gene Smith heads French publications at Headquarters. He spent most of his missionary career in Haiti before helping launch the new work in Martinique. Serving with him in Martinique was Brenda Gould, who had begun her missionary career in Haiti.

There are others whose missionary service in Haiti enriched their ministries. These include Bob Brown, who left Haiti for Nicaragua. From there he went to the Philippines. Michelene Collins started her missionary career in Haiti. She's now married and serving in Malawi. Craig and Gail Zickefoose spent part of a term in Haiti. They now head up Work and Witness in Venezuela.

Through the years, lots of Nazarene young people have gone to Haiti on short mission trips. They've been touched in special ways by Haiti and the Haitian Nazarenes. The list of those young people includes John Seaman, pioneer missionary in French-speaking Africa, as well as myself. In 1970, John and I went to Haiti on a missions field trip for seminary students. Those three weeks in a group led by Dr. Paul Orjala made deep impressions on both of us.

Orjala. Crow. Rich. Read. Weber. Morrow. Smith. And all the others. They went to Haiti to serve. While there they were also served. They went to impart, but they also took in. They went to teach, but they were also taught. The Kingdom is striking back. Its assault force grows stronger as mission fields like Haiti become missionary training and recruiting centers.

The signs of the Messiah are clear. He has come. He is at work.

6

The Poor Are Hearing the Good News

Once-lame men were walking. Blind men were seeing. The deaf started hearing. Even the dead were coming back to life. Such miracles left little doubt that Jesus was Master over the forces of the universe. As Jesus noted these miracles to John's disciples, He was building to a climax. There was a final and supreme proof that God's kingdom had broken in upon the affairs of men. That final, special sign was that *the poor were having the gospel preached to them.* This, says John Wesley, "was the greatest miracle of all."

To us today it may not seem like much of a miracle. We expect to find the poor in and around the church. Two thousand years ago, however, things were different. The great teachers of Rome, Greece, Egypt, and even of the Orient snubbed the poor. Old Testament teaching on God's special care for the downtrodden was clear. Still, the rabbis of Israel seemed repulsed by the poor. In places the Talmud, a collection of Jewish civil and canonical laws, seems contemptuous of the poor.

Jesus was different. Flying in the face of religious tradition, Jesus centered His ministry on the poor. He even went so far as to point out that privileged status for the poor was a sure sign of the Messiah.

Our Lord's words to John's followers did not end with an exclamation of how the high and mighty were falling at His feet. He didn't whip out a list of impressive endorsements from important people and send that to John. Rather He said, "Tell John I'm preaching to the poor." He seemed certain this would convince John of His Messiahship.

Most of Jesus' followers during His earthly ministry were Galilean peasants. Only a handful of those responding to His message had political, religious, or economic clout. This remained true right to the end of the New Testament. The Church grew rapidly in its first decades. Still, to the Caesars, Neros, and Herods of its day, it was a pitiful minority. The Church of Jesus Christ looked like a passel of helpless people of no account. Most new converts were the offscouring and the disinherited of the Roman Empire. From a worldly point of view, the good news of the Kingdom had come to those who had no right to it: the poor.

Caesar and Nero and Herod were wrong, of course. Jesus was the promised Messiah. Today Christianity is the only truly global religion. It has influenced mankind more than any other religion. Yet even today the Church is most vigorous and alive where it targets the disenfranchised rather than the movers and shakers of society. How do we know the Messiah has come? It's because the gospel is being preached to the poor.

I grew up in a Nazarene parsonage in the 1950s. Back then we Nazarenes were "the church across the tracks." Our churches were located in the poor section of town. People looked on us with disdain. Some openly ridiculed us. We bristled at that kind of treatment. We craved some status for our motley collections of day laborers, widows, and short-order cooks.

That's the way the Church of the Nazarene began at the turn of the century, of course. Phineas F. Bresee's burden was a ministry to the poor. That burden led him to found the Church of the Nazarene in Los Angeles.

It's different now. Redemption lift has raised the economic and social level of many Nazarene churches. Unfortunately, our desire for respect in the religious world has sometimes obscured the dangers of wealth and status. From time to time the Holy Spirit has had to call us back to our roots.

Actually, the Nazarenes in most countries still come from the lower economic levels. Don't let that embarrass you. It's a sure sign of the Kingdom in our midst!

The biggest response to Nazarene missionary efforts has come in one of the poorest countries of the world: Haiti. That's significant. It proves that the Kingdom is at work. It confirms that our message and goals still coincide with what the Holy Spirit had in mind when He raised us up at the beginning of this century.

Spontaneous Combustion

One day I was down on Haiti's southern peninsula with District Superintendent Evens Grammont. We were headed to Pestel for a zone rally. Coming down a steep gravel mountain road, we rounded a corner. There, nailed to a tree, was a crude, hand-lettered sign reading "Church of the Nazarene." An arrow pointed down a footpath.

Eyebrows raised, Rev. Grammont turned to me. "I didn't know we had a church there," he said rather matter-of-factly. We continued down the mountain to the seacoast for the rally. After the service, we stood around talking with some of the pastors. We discovered there were two more new churches waiting for the district superintendent to come and formally organize them.

Unusual? Not in Haiti. Such spontaneous combustion is exactly how the Church of the Nazarene has grown there. On

Haiti's parched mountainsides where little else seems to grow, Nazarene churches have sprouted and flourished. Big churches. Little churches. Medium-sized churches. City churches. Village churches. Country churches. Churches with nice buildings. Churches that for 25 years have had only a brush arbor. Nazarene churches: more than 300 of them in all.

Coupled with this explosive church planting is an aggressive evangelistic program involving all churches, both old and new. In fact, in 1984 Haitian Nazarene pastors baptized nearly 3,000 people on one Sunday. That's a story reminiscent of the Day of Pentecost.

What ignites these fires of evangelism and church planting? Why is the Church of the Nazarene spreading so explosively in Haiti? How has it been able to sustain such growth over a prolonged period?

During our first term in Haiti, I asked myself those questions. I've come up with some tentative answers. First, churches are planted in Haiti at the grassroots level. That is, new churches are not planted by missionaries. They're not planted by Haitian district leaders. Rather, most new Nazarene churches in Haiti are planted through initiatives taken by local congregations.

Many Haitian Nazarene churches resemble a mother hen with several little baby chicks. That is, most Nazarene churches in Haiti will supervise one or more "stations" or preaching points. These are places in outlying neighborhoods or other villages where at least one service is held each week. Some of these groups will develop into fully organized churches. Others will remain evangelistic outposts, funneling new converts into the mother church.

Haitian Nazarene pastors seem to echo John Wesley when he said: "The world is my parish." That is, they don't see their ministry goal as being to pastor one specific local church.

Rather, they often see God's call as one to plant churches (with an emphasis on the plural).

The number that Haitian Nazarene pastors point to with the most pride is not their average Sunday School attendance. Nor is it new buildings built or the amount of money raised. It isn't even the number of new converts. The most important statistic to many Haitian pastors is the number of stations they have. A church planting mind-set grips these men.

Another feature of our explosive growth in Haiti is heavy lay involvement. Most stations have lay leaders supervised by the pastor. Laymen even do the preaching in the stations on a rotating basis.

Those new groups we stumbled onto out on the southern peninsula resulted from a layman's work. The Haitian government had sent a Nazarene public school teacher to that area for some practice teaching. There was no Nazarene church in the area. So, during the several months he was there, he started five churches. The gospel was being preached to the poor, and it was being done by a layman. The Messiah has come!

Haitian Nazarenes love evangelizing. Most churches sponsor at least one preaching mission per year. This will be a week-long foray into another village. Sometimes it will be where there is already a Nazarene church. Sometimes it will be into an unreached area. The people will sleep in makeshift quarters, cooking over open fires and going door-to-door witnessing. In the evenings they hold open-air meetings. The results of these missions include churches revived, new churches planted, and new preaching points organized.

In 1987, for example, after district assembly, the Port-de-Paix church sent a group up the mountain to a village called Gashinet. During that preaching mission 19 people found the Lord. These 19 became a core group for a station. By the next district assembly that group of 19 had grown to 60 Christians clamoring for recognition as a fully organized church. Astoundingly, this was not the fruit of a professional evangelist or the district superintendent. It wasn't even the fruit of a veteran pastor. All the work had been done by laymen!

In the mother church itself a layman will often fill the pulpit. This is particularly true of revival meetings. For instance, the ladies' group may have total responsibility for organizing one week-long revival. Everything in the next revival (including the preaching) may be cared for by the young adult group. Our churches occasionally organize 40-day revival meetings with services both morning and evening. The pastor himself may preach in a few of the services. Neighboring pastors may come to preach on a night or two. In most of the services during that nearly six-week period, however, laymen do the preaching.

Many Haitian Nazarene pastors view most of their members as soul winners. There's no small corps of highly trained personal evangelists. Everyone is a personal evangelist! For instance, not long ago I was worshiping with our Pétionville church. Pastor Remy Cherenfant welcomed several first-time visitors to the service. During his warm greeting he told visitors they could talk to anyone about becoming a Christian or joining the church. Any member of the church, he said, stressing *any*, would help them find Christ or be able to answer questions about membership in the Church of the Nazarene.

What Remy Cherenfant said was not unique to the Pétionville Nazarenes. Rather, this every-member-an-evangelist quality is common to Nazarene churches all over Haiti. The poor are having the gospel preached to them. Such preaching is being done, not by a select few, but by the mass of people called Nazarenes.

Much is said about our high-tech age. Ardent fans of technology trumpet its possibilities for accelerating church growth.

Against this background of high hopes for technology, rapid church growth in Haiti has been strictly a low-tech phenomenon. Very little sophisticated mass communications media has been used. Most areas of the country do not have electricity. Travel is often by foot. Even where motor vehicles are available, the roads may be very poor. It can take hours to travel only a few miles. Very few telephones exist outside of Port-au-Prince. The postal system is almost nonexistent.

Haitian Nazarenes do not use these and other tools thought vital for effective outreach in the final decade of the 20th century. Yet they're seeing explosive growth. Without a doubt, one of the reasons for this is the mobilization of every member in evangelistic outreach.

Most church planting in Haiti does not involve large investments of money. Usually no thought is given to providing a permanent building until a station develops into a fully organized church. Up until then, meetings will be held under a brush arbor or in a house. Thus, if a station fails to develop and dies, we've not squandered money in a fruitless effort.

Sometimes new Bible school graduates start a church in a new town. In these cases, General Budget money rents a building and pays some initial salary support. Even in these cases, however, the church planting effort is linked with a new elementary school or a pharmacy/clinic, which help the pastor become self-supporting.

Actually, most of our Haitian churches are self-supporting. Only new Bible college graduates are eligible for salary subsidy, and then only for a maximum of three years. Of course, through Approved Special funds we can help local churches purchase Coleman lanterns, accordions, battery-powered loudspeaker systems, and horses and motorcycles for pastors.

Without a complex structure or a high-powered program, Haitian Nazarenes are reaping an unbelievable harvest. We precise North American missionaries have our pocket calendars with hourly appointment schedules. We keep tidy filing cabinets. We insist on all kinds of complicated report forms. Sometimes we pull our hair out in dismay over what seems to be administrative chaos in places like Haiti. At these times the Lord reminds us that His command was not to keep tidy file cabinets. Rather, He told us to preach the gospel to every person on earth. It's a job the Haitian Nazarenes do very, very well.

Stadium Crusades

The Church of the Nazarene sponsored the first-ever evangelistic crusade in Port-au-Prince's 25,000-seat soccer stadium. That was in 1966. Since then, other groups have used that stadium for crusades. We were the first, however, and what a harvest we reaped. A veteran pastor took some of the converts from that crusade and planted a church. Twenty years later that church, Bel Air, has up to 2,000 to 2,500 in its services. One of the converts in that stadium crusade was a young man named Evens Grammont. Today, Rev. Grammont is superintendent of the Haiti South District. He directs our Haitian Creole radio ministry. Respected by Nazarenes across Haiti, he recently served as our denomination's official spokesperson to the Haitian government.

Another crusade is now in the planning stages. One of the goals would be launching another new church. Services in the stadium would be broadcast live on a network of Christian radio stations. This would allow Nazarenes from all over Haiti to join the crusade.

In 1986 the Church of the Nazarene in Port-de-Paix led in organizing an interdenominational citywide crusade. Much of the fruit from the crusade in that northern coastal city was harvested by that Nazarene church.

Groups of churches throughout Haiti often hold zone rallies or even camp meetings. At one time, about 10 Nazarene churches in the extreme southeastern part of Haiti held a weekend camp meeting. There was some civil unrest in the country. Undaunted, over 1,000 people came to camp meeting. Thirty-five were baptized on Sunday afternoon.

Jesus said, "The kingdom of heaven is like unto a net, that was cast into the sea" (Matt. 13:47, KJV). These crusades and camp meetings, large and small, are visible happenings of our casting our nets. Among the poor of Haiti we've had some good catches!

Sometimes, however, when I begin reeling off church growth figures for Haiti, I'll get disbelieving looks. Those numbers are astounding. The growth has been rapid. Can we trust these statistics? Are they really accurate? Are they inflated to please the missionaries and general leaders?

To answer those questions, you need to visit a Haitian church on Sunday morning. During the first part of the service you'll most likely see an usher pass down the rows. He'll be making check marks on cards held out by many of the people. You see, before a person joins the Church of the Nazarene in Haiti, he usually must be baptized. He cannot be baptized if he does not regularly attend services after his conversion. Attendance will probably also be required at a new converts' class. These classes often meet during Sunday School for six weeks or so. Ushers mark their cards to check their attendance record. Many of the churches also use attendance cards for full members to encourage their faithfulness as well.

In addition we have discovered that converts in some of the more remote preaching points sometimes do not get counted in membership statistics. Some stations having only weeknight services are too far from the mother church building for people to participate in its regular services. The mother church sometimes forgets to put these converts from the station on its rolls. So they miss getting counted in annual reports. Such groups of people are really Nazarenes. While they don't get counted, their presence helps balance out any deadwood we may have in existing churches.

Work and Witness

An important issue in church planting anywhere is providing facilities for worship, education, and evangelism. People need places to meet. The buildings used by Haitian Nazarenes come in all types. They range from tiny, cramped rooms to spacious, barnlike buildings. Some are brightly painted. Others are simple brush arbors with no walls to paint. A few have tile floors. Many have only dirt.

In Haiti the local Nazarenes almost always build their first building as a brush-arbor-type structure. In a deforested country like Haiti, big trees to make rafters and beams are not available. So as the group expands beyond the size of a small house, they have to go to concrete blocks and mortar and steel. Costs for these materials usually exceed their financial capabilities. Haitian banks don't loan money to churches. So these Haitian Nazarenes have to look for outside help.

In the early days of our work in Haiti that help came from Alabaster funds. Recently, most of it has had to come from Work and Witness teams. A limited amount of Alabaster money has also been available to help purchase property.

Scott and Pamela Hannay work full-time with construction and the Work and Witness teams. Our rapid growth in Haiti forces a hectic pace of church construction. In one five-week period district superintendents dedicated four new church buildings built by Work and Witness teams. Our district superintendents have one gripe against our Work and Witness missionaries. They complain that they haven't figured out a way to work 24 hours a day. The list of our construction needs is long. Right now the districts have more than 100 projects on their high-priority lists. Each new church organized means a building needed sometime in the future.

Their 50 Percent?

The World Mission Division has some rules governing church construction on mission fields. One rule says that the local Nazarenes must give at least one-half of what it takes to build their building. They can't get a bank loan. So how do they pay for their 50 percent?

Some creative ways are used to ensure compliance with the rule. An interesting story happened out on La Gonâve a few years ago. A village called Grand Source lies two hours' walk up the mountain above a coastal fishing village. I've walked up and back down that rock-strewn trail a couple of times. Those Nazarenes carried concrete blocks on their heads on that two-hour walk up the mountain to build their church. Computed solely in dollars and cents, it would be hard to argue that they'd given 50 percent. They did not pay for the blocks. Still, those days of climbing that mountain, carrying those concrete blocks one by one, seems a bigger investment than the cash gift they'd received from an American church.

High in the mountains along the southern coast is a rural village called Fond Melon. The Nazarenes there had to get building materials up a long, winding footpath following a stream up a steep valley. Missionary Charles Morrow told me they approached the problem like American churches approach their building projects. They took pledges! Some folks pledged to carry pieces of tin. Others pledged to carry a certain number of concrete blocks. Still others pledged to carry so much sand. One lady pledged to make several horse trips to carry up the sacks of cement.

I remember a dedication service in a mountain village called Lachaud. The building had been nearly completed by a Work and Witness team a few weeks earlier. The finishing touches had been completed. So a special Sunday morning dedication service led by the district superintendent was planned. He asked me to be present on behalf of the work team. During the Saturday evening and Sunday morning I was at Lachaud, I thought a lot about the mission policy's 50 percent clause. I'm convinced that what counted as the Haitians' 50 percent was a good deal more than the American Work and Witness team's 50 percent.

Let me explain: Lachaud is two hours' walk from the end of the road. The path that began where I parked my jeep was a mountain trail running straight up a mountainside. It was steep and covered with loose gravel. That Saturday afternoon I had trouble just getting myself up it.

The building we dedicated Sunday morning was a prefabricated metal one. I knew that every piece of steel had gone up that trail on somebody's head. The 100-pound sacks of cement for the floor and foundation had gone up on the backs of horses belonging to members of the church. Schoolchildren carried the sand up in dishpans on their heads. There's no spring on top of the mountain. To get water, people from the village have to walk back down that trail about half an hour. All the water for mixing cement (and for baths for Work and Witness team members) had gone up that trail on somebody's head.

Sunday morning we had a great dedication service. The people sang gladly. They clapped for joy. They listened intently to God's Word. We thanked the Lord for this tangible sign of the Kingdom's intrusion into that area.

After the service, we started back down that steep trail. I felt my toes pushing deeper and deeper into the ends of my hiking boots. Finally I felt them starting to curl under. As we neared the bottom, I wondered how long it would take for those toes to uncurl. I also knew I would need to order new parts for my knees. My ankles were going to need replacing.

I felt exhausted when we reached the bottom. Yet all I had done was get myself up that trail and back down again. I thought about the materials for that church. Lachaud Nazarenes made that tortuous trip over and over, carrying sheets of roofing, steel bars, cement, sand, water, and even supplies for the Work and Witness team.

The biggest problem was a heavy gasoline generator/welder that needed to go up to the jobsite. Missionary Bob Say had built a carrying frame for the welder. It vaguely resembled a wheelbarrow with handles coming out both ends. He placed handles on both ends and one large wheel under the center of the heavy machine. He hoped that would enable at least four men to push and pull it up that trail. It was still bulky and heavy. Climbing that steep trail with it was not going to be easy.

The Work and Witness team from Wichita, Kans., climbed the steep mountain trail their first night. They carried little more than their toothbrushes and some food supplies. The generator/welder had been left at the bottom of the trail. Members of the Haitian congregation were going to try to bring it up.

By the time the Work and Witness team got up to the village, it was late afternoon. Exhausted from their climb, they sat eating supper. They had raised $5,000 above their expenses to buy materials for this building. Now they began to wonder if they could put it together without a welder. They barely managed to get themselves up that mountainside. The welder/

generator? No way. They knew how heavy it was. The more they thought about it, the more impossible the task of getting it up the mountain seemed. They had loaded it on the pickup back in Port-au-Prince and struggled to get it off at the end of the road. Carry it up that path? No way. Someone mentioned how easy it would be if they only had a helicopter.

Supper ended. Darkness fell. Then, from far away, singing came floating up the steep trail. Gradually the sounds came closer and closer. Finally, over the top came a group of men dragging that generator/welder. The Americans stared in disbelief. Then tears came to eyes as they saw the cut and bruised arms and legs of the men struggling with that machine.

The generator/welder showed signs of having taken a tumble or two. Obviously it had been a tough climb. In spite of the new dents and scratches, it started up with the first pull on the starter rope.

The building went up in record time. The most amazing thing for everyone, however, was not how quick the building went up. The biggest story was the arrival of that portable welding machine.

Construction completed, the American team packed their belongings. They started down the trail, slipping and sliding. As they went over the crest, they looked back. There were the men of the church discussing how to start back down the trail with that generator/welder. Sure enough, hours later the men waiting with a pickup at the end of the road looked up. There were the men of the church lugging that welding machine. What had gone up had indeed come down.

Did Lachaud give their 50 percent? Did they obey the official rule? I'm not certain you can compute it easily in dollars and cents. Sunday after the dedication service I slithered and slid down that mountain trail from Lachaud. As I thought about that building project, tears welled up in my eyes. Lachaud's 50 percent?

Somehow their contributions seemed to carry a higher price tag than the work team's $5,000. Certainly some Americans had given freely to buy those materials. Perhaps you could even call it "sacrificial giving." The Americans, however, had given out of their abundance. These folks from Lachaud were malnourished and plagued by intestinal parasites, malaria, and other health problems. They had done what the healthy Americans did not think possible. In doing so, they had literally given of their lifeblood to build a place to preach about their Messiah. Christ did come. He is present today. The commitment of the Lachaud Nazarenes is proof of that.

Like a Prairie Fire

While growing up in southeastern Oklahoma, I remember seeing prairie fires. One stands out in my mind. Several fields had already been burned by the time I arrived. The wind drove the flames through the tall grass like waves coming up on a beach. Farmers tried to make firebreaks. It was no use. The wind blew the sparks over the bare strips. As the fire approached the edge of one field, they prayed that the gravel road would stop it. It didn't. The wind blew burning straw across the road. Off the fire went, blazing through the next field.

The Holy Spirit sparked a flame in the hearts of Haitian Nazarenes. Today it resembles that prairie fire. Satan tried to keep that fire confined to one little Caribbean nation. But he failed badly.

Haiti's dire economic distress has turned many of its people into the wanderers of the Caribbean, indeed of the Western world. Selling everything they have to buy airline or boat tickets, they endanger their lives and risk the wrath of immigration officials in the United States and other countries.

Some of those Haitians trying to emigrate to other countries are Nazarenes. Victims of racial and national prejudice where they've gone, they've clung tenaciously to their faith. They've witnessed to it. They've sought to convert others. Fiercely loyal, these Haitians have tried to plant the Church of the Nazarene wherever they've gone. God has turned economic misfortune into a force for spreading the gospel!

Haitian Nazarenes have planted churches in countries like France, Canada, Suriname, Venezuela, and the United States. Fifty percent of the Nazarenes in the Bahamas are Haitian. Nazarene work in the Dominican Republic began in the mid-1970s. We have watched in wonder at rapid Nazarene growth there. Few people know, however, that 50 percent of the Nazarenes in the Dominican Republic are Haitian. Five of the 15 world regions of the Church of the Nazarene have Haitian churches! In the New York area, in central and south Florida, in eastern Maryland, Haitian Nazarene immigrants get together and start churches. They eventually get discovered by the district and are officially organized. The prairie fire is out of control. The gospel is being preached to the poor. The Kingdom is striking back!

Such spontaneous, rapid growth inspires Nazarenes in other countries. In 1987 the Nazarene Bible College campus near Port-au-Prince hosted the Caribbean Regional Conference. Delegates came to fellowship. They came to plan strategies. They hoped to cement Caribbean unity. Perhaps most of all they came to partake of the Haitian Nazarene spirit. Inspired by a firsthand look at the work of the Holy Spirit through the Haitian Nazarenes, these Caribbean leaders set some lofty goals. One of those goals was "95 by 95." By this they meant reaching 95,000 full members in the Caribbean Region by 1995.

The poor are having the gospel preached to them. The Messiah has come.

7

Conclusion

Jesus said His kingdom would appear insignificant as it emerged. It would at first, He said, seem no more than a tiny mustard seed. Not at all impressive. The prophets predicted people wouldn't even recognize the Kingdom at first. Isaiah said that the Messiah would be "despised and rejected" (53:3). Jesus came to people who were expecting a Messiah. They did not recognize Him; He just did not seem impressive enough.

To some looking on today, God's kingdom may not inspire awe. Don't be caught napping. The Kingdom is present. It is growing in presence and power. I've glimpsed some mighty Kingdom feats in Haiti. Today the Kingdom is at work there as well as elsewhere. In Haiti, it is giving sight to the blind, cleansing the lepers, making the deaf to hear, and making the lame to walk. Most important of all, it is giving the Good News to the poor.

As I've watched the Holy Spirit at work in Haiti, I always come away reassured that on the day of the Resurrection, Jesus will remove all disorders and blemishes from our bodies. He will clothe us in immortal health, beauty, and glory. That's our hope. This brutal, cruel world will pass away. It will be replaced by a reign of peace. Defaced beauty will be restored. Wounds will be healed. All sorrows will be lifted.

Around the globe, we're getting a foretaste of this. Christ is at the Father's right hand. Today the Lord of Lords and King of Kings offers His invincible power to His Church.

The Messiah has come. We have seen the signs of His work. The Kingdom is striking back.

Nazarene Missionaries to Haiti

'50   '60   '70   '80   '90

Orjala, Paul and Mary
Alstott, Charles and Ida
Condor, Max and Mary
Vanciel, Brian and Evelyn
Rich, Harry and Marion
Smith, Gene and Catherine
DePasquale, James and Mary
Crow, Walter and Linda
Borden, Nancy
Devore, Elvin and Evelyn
Ford, Lois (Rodeheaver)
Brown, Bob and Louise
Ford, David
Gould, Brenda
Read, Terry and Joan
Morrow, Charles and Joyce
Weber, Steve and Linda
Van Beek, Jeanine
Hannay, Carolyn Parsons
Taylor, Dave and Pat
Larrabee, Michelene Collins
Wilson, Larry and Martha
Hannay, Scott
Burge, John and Martha
Culbertson, Howard and Barbara
Johnston, Trevor and Mary
Dawson, Bill and Martha
Say, Bob and Nancy
Zickefoose, Craig and Gail
D'Amico, Judi
Hannay, Pamela Grant
Ketchum, Terry and Kathy

His kingdom has broken chains of disease, madness, sin, and death. His kingdom's invasion of this world has opened blinded eyes and given hope to the oppressed. Whatever the sources of human heartache, God in Christ has sought to destroy them.

Penetrating the darkened corners of our world has not been easy. We fight amid the rubble of hate, injustice, disease, and violence. Often the battle rages at what seem to be the very doors of hell itself. At hell's gates is precisely where Jesus told Peter that the Church—the missionary people of the Kingdom—would triumph (Matt. 16:18). Triumphs over the effects of the Fall may sometimes seem partial and insignificant. Still, each victory points to the Kingdom's coming final and complete conquest.

Along the way there have been doubters and scoffers. To some, real Kingdom miracles never seem spectacular enough. That's nothing new. When Jesus was here, His miracles did not convince everyone either. So we can't be too hard on modern-day doubters. Even Jesus' cousin, John, needed some reassurances of His Messiahship.

Around the turn of this century, the Holy Spirit raised up a revival movement called the Church of the Nazarene. Today, sanctified believers who belong to this movement preach the good news of the Kingdom in more than 90 world areas. I'm part of that movement. In our midst the blind have received sight. We've seen dying people cured. The lame have walked. One of our 16 Articles of Faith boldly proclaims God's miraculous healing powers. To top it all off, we've sometimes been scorned as a church that preaches to the poor. We believe Jesus is the Messiah. We've seen the signs of His kingdom's presence.

In Haiti some 30,000 Nazarenes see daily encounters between God's sovereign reign and Satan's evil hordes. Holy Spirit-inspired ministries of Haitian Nazarenes include medical work and economic aid. We're aggressively evangelizing and planting churches in Haiti. Our education program includes elementary and secondary schools as well as training for pastors and evangelists. The Kingdom is striking back. We're convinced (doubters and scoffers notwithstanding) that this Jesus in whose name and under whose power we preach is the Christ, the promised Messiah.

2

The Blind Are Seeing

Blindness. It tends to make men dependent. It sometimes reduces them to beggars. In Jesus' day, blind people were common in Palestine. They still are. Why? Well, blame the glaring sun, large amounts of dust in the air, flies, and such diseases as smallpox, malaria, and highly infectious ophthalmia.

Was it by chance that Jesus referred to blindness in His response to John's disciples? I don't think so. Opening blind eyes was one definite sign of Messiahship. As Old Testament prophets spoke of the end times and coming new age, they talked of blind eyes that would be opened. Had Jesus not brought sight to the blind, He would not have been the long-awaited Savior.

Jesus healed many people whose lack of physical eyesight kept them in darkness. Blindness was, in fact, the affliction Jesus healed most often. A good example is blind Bartimaeus whom Jesus met on the Jericho road. That day Jesus gave him sight (Mark 10:46-52).

Did Jesus limit himself to healing only *physical* blindness? Look again at the Gospels, and you'll see that Jesus also dealt with spiritual blindness. Once He warned that "the blind lead the blind" (Matt. 15:14, KJV). He didn't mean physical blindness but religious leaders whose lack of spiritual insight and even sinful pride blinded them.

So, as Jesus spoke to John's disciples, He doubtless thought of Old Testament passages such as Isa. 29:18: "Out of gloom and darkness the eyes of the blind will see." Viewed in context, such Old Testament verses refer to spiritual, intellectual, and moral blindness more than they do to actual physical blindness. As God's kingdom continues to strike back today, sight in both senses—physical and spiritual—is being restored.

A blind beggar touched by Jesus struggled to explain what had happened to him. Finally he blurted out: "Once I was blind but now I can see" (John 9:25, Williams). To many Haitians touched by the Kingdom today, that explains what happened to them. Once they were blind. Now they can see. The Messiah has come. He is opening blinded eyes. The Kingdom is striking back.

Used Glasses, Anyone?

Not long ago my mother sent her 100th pair of used eyeglasses to Dr. Paul Gamertsfelder. One hundred pairs? No, my mother doesn't discard eyeglasses that fast. Rather, she collects them from friends all over central Oklahoma. Then she boxes them up to mail to Dr. Gamertsfelder, a Nazarene optometrist in Ohio.

When those glasses arrive from my mother and others like her, Dr. Gamertsfelder and his staff check and label them. Each year Dr. Gamertsfelder and his colleague, Dr. Paul Mason, spend their annual vacations in Haiti. There they use their skills and training and those old eyeglasses to restore clear vision to Haitians with sight problems.

Out in rural villages, with an eye chart thumbtacked to a coconut tree, these optometrists see as many as 200 people in